monsoonbooks

INVISIBLE TRADE

Gerrie Lim is the author of *Inside the Outsider*, a collection of his rock star interviews, and he is currently the International Correspondent for *AVN Online* (www.avnonline.com). He graduated in 1987 from the University of Southern California with a Master of Arts degree in Print Journalism, and has written for *Billboard*, *Details*, *Harper's Bazaar*, *Elle*, *Playboy*, the *San Diego Union-Tribune*, the *South China Morning Post*, *The Wall Street Journal*, and *The Asian Wall Street Journal*.

He spends his time in both Singapore and Los Angeles.

Gerrie Lim

INVISIBLE TRADE

High-class sex for sale in Singapore

monsoon

monsoonbooks

First published in 2004
by Monsoon Books Pte Ltd
Blk 106 Jalan Hang Jebat #02–14
Singapore 139527
www.monsoonbooks.com.sg

ISBN 981-05-1033-0

Printed in Singapore

09 08 07 06 05   4 5 6 7 8 9

For P.H.

"my two-dollar bill"

Contents

Preface   9

Part One: Courtesan Confidential

The Mongolian Strangler   13
Walking The Dog   26
White Diamonds   42
Asian Affairs   59

Part Two: Different Strokes

Her Heart Will Go On   83
Boys In The Hood   105
Victoria's Secrets   124

Part Three: Risqué Business

Girls, Food, Lodging   149
Daughters Of The Tenth Muse   175
Invisible Trade   193

Acknowledgments   203
Suggested Reading   206
Permissions   208

Preface

This book was initially inspired by *Speed Tribes: Days and Nights With Japan's Next Generation* by Karl Taro Greenfeld, in particular a chapter called "Jackie: The Hostess," about the lives of American girls who work as bar hostesses in Tokyo. I would like to thank Karl for his informal complicity and sagely advice.

Like *Speed Tribes*, this is not a work of fiction but most of the names have been changed. I am immensely grateful to all the interviewees for allowing me access to their secret world. A number of escorts and other sex workers were composited into the "characters" found in the chapters. I am also grateful beyond measure to the escort agency owners who willingly granted me interviews and allowed me to interview their girls. Their names have also been changed, upon their request.

Also, for obvious reasons, none of the names of the major hotels have been divulged, nor the names of clients. Should anyone reading this book come to recognize themselves in a particular anecdote or episode, I can only offer my apologies for any embarrassment caused. This book is not meant at all to dissuade you from your lifestyle.

PART ONE

Courtesan Confidential

The Mongolian Strangler

Politics hadn't stopped prostitution;
it had complicated it, taken the fun out of it
and made it assume disguises.

—Paul Theroux, *Saint Jack*

It's nine o'clock in Singapore, a typical balmy night in the
tropics. Humidity hangs heavily in the air as Jasmine hails
a taxi into town. It's time to go to work.

She's going to strangle a man again.

Philip's already waiting when she reaches the hotel on
Orchard Road. He's just flown in from his office in Tokyo.
He called the escort agency from his cellphone while waiting
for his bags at Changi Airport, requesting for Jasmine once
more. Where some might view this as impatience, Philip
prefers to think of it as anticipation. He knows what he
wants, so why delay the gratification? Book the girl as soon
as you get in. Lock and load. Crosshairs on the target.

Philip likes this tall, lithe girl from Mongolia, with her jet-black hair and long, strong legs. And strong legs are essential for what he has in mind. Philip thinks she's easily impressed, especially with his suave looks, designer labels, and taste for fine wines. Tonight, he's already made a start on a 2000 Joseph Phelps Insignia Napa Valley, S$250 a bottle, a score of ninety-two from *Wine Spectator*. But Californian Cabernet isn't what Jasmine really comes here for, and she's not that easily impressed. After all, at S$600 an hour, she's worth a few bottles of those, though she feeds a distinctly different appetite.

No fancy dinner, no small talk. Jasmine reclines on the carpet fully clothed as Philip undresses himself. Totally naked now, he rests his neck on her thighs and signals for her to begin. Ten minutes later he reaches climax and they're done.

Auto-asphyxiation normally requires a man to loop a noose around his neck with a rope or a belt. The choking sensation produces a terrific rush when he masturbates to climax. But Philip isn't going the way of Michael Hutchence of INXS, who did just that and was found dead in a Sydney hotel room. That's why he needs Jasmine, who chokes him—with her thighs.

If by chance he's quaffed too much wine, he'll slap her leg gently. This is their signal, meaning she's supposed to stop.

"He likes me to strangle him so he can reach a really intense orgasm, and he always comes," explains Jasmine. "When I'm doing it, I'm usually dressed and he's the one who's naked. I wear jeans. I can't wear any kinds of pants that can be slippery. They have to have a grip."

Jasmine, now twenty-eight, first came to Singapore eight years ago when a friend enrolled her in a computer programming class. She learned the basics in Singapore before completing her computer science studies in Melbourne, Australia, funded in part by her escorting tips. Until she met her current agency boss in Singapore six years ago, Jasmine had never worked in any area of the sex industry.

"In the beginning, every job was difficult for me," she recalls. "I wouldn't say I'm very experienced even now, but I know what I'm doing. Once I made the decision to do this, it took about six months for me to get used to it and a year to get to the point where I could feel confident in my abilities. In my opinion, that's slow compared to some other girls. In the early days I wouldn't even know which hotel to go to and when I got there, I'd get lost. I got lost at the first big hotel I had to go to. I didn't know which of the three wings the room was in! I went back to the agency crying. They sent another girl. I lost that client."

People outside the sex industry suspect there's sex involved in escorting, but they don't know how much. The average booking lasts for three hours but this is for escorting only: dinner, dancing, karaoke, or maybe even a shopping trip. Sex usually takes place afterwards, if requested by the client, and is always negotiated separately after the initial booking time has elapsed. The carnal congress can last as long as the client's money allows. "It depends," Jasmine reveals. "It can last from thirty minutes to an hour. Usually, they like to finish pretty quickly but I can get them going again after that. That's how I get repeat customers—I'd say 40 percent of mine are repeats. But I had one guy who took a very long time, almost one hour, to get fully aroused. When it comes to sex, I usually don't mind if the guy is good and can really last a long time, because I can last a long time myself. But it's hard if it takes a long time for him to even get erect. I had to do a lot of touching and a lot of encouraging."

Such techniques require learning, outside the classroom. "Sometimes I watch porno movies," Jasmine giggles. "You can get them even in Mongolia, believe it or not, especially in the capital, Ulan Bator, where I grew up." Actually, pornographic material is also available in Singapore, even though it's officially banned; everything is for sale if you know where to look. Lucky for Jasmine, since she intends to remain in Singapore rather than return to Mongolia. "If you're shopping in Ulan Bator, you have to choose between ethnic art, ethnic dresses, cashmere sweaters, and chess sets. And if you want to mail a letter, you have to personally go to the post office; mailboxes on the streets don't exist." Not the sort of place where a girl gets paid to strangle a guy for his sheer sexual pleasure then—particularly with her thighs.

"I have also done strangling with my arms but I don't think I'm strong enough for that," Jasmine concedes. "I have had guys ask me to try to use my arms. Some girls prefer to do that, but not me. I'm more comfortable doing it with my legs. When I'm done, I don't even have to clean him up. He just goes off to the toilet himself and I'm done."

The S$600 Jasmine earns from Philip is not bad at all for ten minutes' work. Agency rules are such that Philip has to pay the entire hourly rate, even if it took a mere ten minutes. Strangulation is S$600 an hour, and anything kinkier, like whipping or spanking, starts at S$700 to S$1,000 an hour. As Jasmine leaves the room with S$600 in cash, she gets a peck on the cheek from Philip. She ambles down the corridor and into the elevator as Philip returns to his Joseph Phelps.

Jasmine's had sex in three rooms of this hotel in the past year. Only one strangulation, but there have been a few more in other hotels, other rooms. The money sure is good, assuming you don't kill anyone.

When an ambitious, adventurous gent named Sir Thomas Stamford Raffles "discovered" this tiny Southeast Asian island in 1819, claiming it for the British Crown, he envisioned it as a geographical gateway between East and West. The years since have seen it flourish commercially, though some would shake their heads in disbelief if they knew what else went on behind closed doors.

Some aspects of the sex trade are well known, with much made of it by the foreign news media—approximately 190 foreign correspondents from eighty-five news agencies are based in Singapore and thirty-two foreign publications are printed here. But much of what goes on is not reported in the local or foreign press and its existence would no doubt come as a surprise to many Singapore residents as well as foreigners.

Singapore has enjoyed nearly forty years of prosperity following independence in 1965, first from the British Empire and then from the Malaysian Federation. But as many cultural observers have noticed, rapid modernization has come at a heavy price: the quashing of political dissent by a single-party government and the censorship of mass media. Italian travel writer Tiziano Terzani wrote of Singapore in *A Fortune-Teller Told Me: Earthbound Travels in the Far East*, that "behind all its alluring and welcoming shopping malls, shopping arcades and shopping centers, it remains a police state, a society shot through with a subtle fear."

Interestingly, Singapore's tourism industry, a critical element given the country's lack of natural resources, spawned a quick-turnover visitor market together with some of the best five-star hotels in the world. The Ritz-Carlton Millenia Singapore houses art by Frank Stella and David Hockney, its 608 rooms good enough for the likes of entertainers Mariah Carey and Alanis Morissette. Or the more famous Raffles Hotel, which hosted luminaries Elizabeth Taylor, Michael Jackson, and John Lennon, now refurbished with an exclusive shopping arcade attached.

Escorts like Jasmine only work five-star hotel rooms. Their affluent clientele are disposable men with disposable income, answering the higher callings of their libido. And why not? Should anyone be surprised? The sexually voracious male is hardly a stranger to these parts. The late Helmut Newton, the celebrated erotic photographer from Berlin, devotes quite a lot of space to Singapore in his recently published autobiography (called *Autobiography*), in which he recalls his strange tenure here from 1938 to 1940, while fleeing Nazi Germany en route to Australia. Newton namechecked notorious pimping spots in Singapore like the old Change Alley (incorrectly calling it "Chaney Alley"). Paul Theroux, of course, wrote the most famous book about prostitution in Singapore, his 1973 novel *Saint Jack*, in which he describes how girls are brought in, "docked at Pasir Panjang behind a palm grove," rather than at the more heavily policed piers of Collyer Quay and Jardine Steps. The protagonist, an American refugee named Jack Flowers, flees a probable drug bust in Boston only to end up pimping in Singapore for fourteen years. His shenanigans include running the Paradise Gardens "hotel" for visiting U.S. military personnel—a revolving-door deployment of redneck yahoos and sad sacks, fatally assigned to the Vietnam conflagration but fatefully, pleasurably, grappling with girls named Florence, Soo-hin, and Annapurna, and etching forever into the annals of famous literary place-names some of the local streets like Adam Road and Jalan Kembang Mati.

Flowers naturally exalts his vocation, describing it as "perfect candour, private discovery, the enactment of the white bachelor's fantasy, the next best thing to marrying a sweet obedient Chinese girl. I could provide, without danger, the ultimate souvenir: the experience, in the flesh, of fantasy."

Thirty years later, prostitution remains legal in Singapore, but only because it is regulated. In the East Coast enclave of Geylang, legal brothels exist but the girls must ply their trade only in the designated houses, never out on the streets. They carry yellow-colored identification cards, marking them as legal sex workers.

Yet a whole other subculture is thriving, with no need for government intervention and yellow cards. It thrives on discretion and secrecy. The girls answer advertisements in the papers calling for "confidential hostesses"; the word "escort" is not permitted in newspaper advertising, though it is in the Singapore *Yellow Pages* phone book. At last count, there were twenty-two pages of escort agencies, some of which pay S$40,000 to S$60,000 per advertisement. Most of the girls are extremely well turned-out. Hair and make-up just right, backless halter dresses and skirts just above the knee. Swarovski pendants, Louis Vuitton handbags and definitely no gimcrack jewelry. Many of them are well-read (Xaviera Hollander's *The Happy Hooker* is mandatory, Louise Brown's more academic *Sex Slaves* is passed around) and some are even students, pursuing degrees in business administration and computer programming.

And, because they're not mere sex-doll bimbos, they command atypical prices. Yellow-card girls will service a guy for only S$50. One escort received a S$500 tip for simply accompanying a gentleman to breakfast at 7.30 a.m. No sex was involved. He merely wanted the company of a pretty girl as he babbled on about mutual funds. This particular escort was perfect because she was pursuing a Master's degree in Finance and wanted someday to be a financial controller.

As Terence, the owner of an escort agency in Singapore, succinctly puts it, the idea is to simply "facilitate companionship"; the client pays a booking fee to secure a girl, and "what happens after dinner is between him and the girl, I don't need to know." The client, of course, pays extra hourly rates to "extend the booking." Elsewhere, karaoke hostesses and massage parlors provide sexual services behind closed doors. Things can get interesting in the private rooms of karaoke bars, to the tune of S$300 for a bottle of Chivas Regal, S$300 for sex. Or S$100 for a blow job, if that's all you can afford. A karaoke bar hostess will sit on your lap, pull her top down and let you play with her. She'll nonchalantly lean over to get a cigarette, allowing you to slip your hand inside her G-string. At some of these places, the evening's drink tab can hit S$2,000 for just two guys, up to S$8,000 if you've brought a small entourage. And that's not including tips for the girls.

There are, Terence says, too many girls from mainland China now, "spoiling the market" because they're avaricious—rude and crude, grasping and greedy. Not the kind of image that the upscale escort agencies want to project. None of the high-end agencies will ever employ these girls, who end up at the flashy karaoke bars or in the rinky-dinky massage parlors, which are also drolly called "health centers."

And then, there's the newest phenomenon, the Natashas and Zitas, the Russian and Eastern European girls who work out of three-star hotels with their private pimps. In these times, through the unraveling economic tailspin, more girls have started coming in from Uzbekistan, usually via neighboring Malaysia.

Svetlana comes to Singapore and instantly becomes Sandy, because she has sandy-blond hair. She's drop-dead gorgeous and could be mistaken for a fashion model. Some of these girls actually are, moonlighting as escorts for a few weeks before hurtling across the Causeway, to get their passports stamped with "social visit passes." They always tell you they're here for "tourism." They're walking down Orchard Road, Scotts Road, past Takashimaya and into the triangle demarcated by Hotel Grand Central, Cuppage Plaza, and Orchard Plaza, where the karaoke bars are doing their usual roaring business.

But these girls aren't going to pour drinks or light cigarettes or offer hot towels to drunken Japanese executives. They're traipsing into hotel rooms and private condos with all the swank and swagger of the newly enfranchised. Some of them are merely in long-term rebellion against their straight-laced, middle-class backgrounds, while others, like Sandy, do it because they really need the money, and then find themselves stuck. The money is too good, too easily gained, and in no time the shopping, gambling, or drug bills mount up. Working girls keep on working, to finance an opulent lifestyle.

So spins the wheel of fate, surely as money makes the world go round. But only the most sexually repressed person would hate them for being so beautiful and so bold.

Especially in this newly globalized world, where geopolitical borders cannot hamper their invisible trade.

Ask Sandy. She'll tell you that at the end of the day, she'll do what needs to be done because she needs the money. Hers is a quiet desperation born of pain, an unyielding pathos her rich clients don't need to understand. Her high heels and sexy clothes are for a costume party of the mind; part fun, part illusion.

"You would know, if you have ever been to Tashkent," she says. "I don't want to be poor anymore."

Walking The Dog

Look I'm standing naked before you
Don't you want more than my sex
I can scream as loud as your last one
But I can't claim innocence

—Tori Amos, *Leather*

"The first time I did it, I cried," explains Emily. "For everybody, there is always a first time, where you get upset. Where you feel like you're dirty, you're selling your body." She flicks stray bangs off her forehead, revealing a furrowed brow, and lodges a fresh smoke between her pursed lips. She's twenty-eight years old, a Chinese Singaporean who grew up in the old pre-war shophouse district around Lavender Street.

"In the early days, I had problems talking with the customers. The first time I dressed up, I was terrible. I dressed like an *ah lian*, a village girl. And I talked very loudly. Sapphire, my agency owner, guided me a lot. My hair was terrible, all bunched up and curly like Maggi Mee instant noodles, and Sapphire told me it was ugly and made me straighten it. She told me not to talk as if I was going to have a fight, or to wear platforms or tight pants. She made me look through magazines. She taught me how to talk politely to the customers."

Sapphire laughs when reminded of this. "When Emily went out on her early assignments, her service was always bad. It was like hit-and-run, and the customers complained. I told her, 'How can you go to a customer and speak like a gangster?' She was so rude. I told her, 'The next time a customer complains, I won't use you anymore.' She's improved a lot since then."

Well, she must have, since she now commands S$700 to S$1,000 an hour, in part because she does the jobs the other girls won't do. Group sex, bondage and domination, whipping and spanking, hot wax and other forms of unusual punishment. There's a slight twist to her lips, a subtle pout that hints of cruelty, which lends a menacing aura to her not unattractive visage, one blessed with all the known attributes of classical Chinese beauty. Emily has an oval face with eyes and nose perfectly proportioned, set off with the kind of long black hair and pale, porcelain skin so very prized by Western men. A lot of her customers come from cities like London and Boston, places she has never been to and could barely find on a map ten years ago, when she began escorting at the age of nineteen.

"On my first job I was very frightened and didn't know what to do. I had to go straight to a hotel and I didn't know who would be answering the door. I didn't know how to do a massage or how to talk to a strange guy. The agency I was working for then didn't train me or anything. On that first job, when I knocked on the hotel room door, I actually covered the peephole so the man wouldn't see me!

"But the evening went smoothly. He was a foreign guy, an *ang moh*, a white man. Looked a bit like Brad Pitt. I didn't even have sex with him. He wanted to but I told him I was too nervous! He was nice about it. I finished the three hours of escorting and left. We just went out to dinner and talked. I remember that I didn't eat anything. I was terrified that he might drug my drink or my food. You never know what might happen when you're out with a total stranger. I even went on a job after that where they sent me to Brunei. But I made a U-turn and came back. I had never been on a plane before, I was so scared and I cried and cried.

"They were very nice about it. They paid me S$1,000 and sent me back. One thousand dollars, just to make a U-turn! But soon I started being able to have sex, with no problems. Nothing kinky, just straight sex. Now I've matured to the point where I will do anything."

Now, Emily works as a masseuse in a women's slimming salon during the day, and escorting is merely her night job. "I do body massage for ladies. I do facials too. I put mudpacks on their faces, scrub them, put them in machines that break down cellulite, and wrap them up like mummies. I went to beautician school too. Then, a customer gave me $5,000 to attend a make-up course. I went because he paid for it. But I realized I was more interested in beauty than in make-up."

So what's a beautician like her doing in a place like this? It's a rhetorical question made poignant by the fact that the area she grew up in happens to lie amid the very districts where the world's oldest profession first took root in Singapore. Large-scale commercial movements of women for the purpose of pleasure took place in the late 19th century, whereby Chinese girls were sent to Singapore, Malaysia, and Thailand to satisfy the growing numbers of male migrant laborers eking out a living in the ports. The historian James

Francis Warren, in his book *Ah Ku and Karayuki-San: Prostitution in Singapore, 1870-1940,* notes that "the economic development of Singapore favored prostitution as the male population of the city greatly outnumbered the females: the gap was 1 female to 14 males in 1860 and this gender imbalance was to continue for the next seventy years."

Sex for sale is, of course, best known in Thailand, but Emily's place in the pecking order is at the opposite end of the spectrum from the hapless Burmese girls who still work the cheapest Bangkok brothels. No, Emily spends her evenings ensconced in five-star hotels, sipping Champagne and surveying the scenery from penthouse suites. There might well be a Japanese executive at hand who has paid handsomely for her services. And not necessarily for sex.

"One Japanese guy wanted me to treat him like a dog," Emily recalls. "He wanted me to see what was in the fridge and feed it to him. I would drip chocolate onto a saucer and make him eat it. Squash his head with my leg and make him eat a biscuit off the floor. Whip him. Walk him up and down on a leash. I brought my own dog leash, tied it around his neck, and made him walk around the whole hotel room. Then he had to pee like a dog, on the carpet. No sex. He masturbated himself.

"This was at seven o'clock in the morning! I got the call from the agency at 6.30 a.m. It took one hour, and I was done by eight o'clock." She takes another drag of her cigarette.

Escorting is an outcall business, so Emily has to go out to work, unlike call girls who'll receive calls and then customers at their residences, like those fabulous New York call girls who work out of their Upper East Side apartments. "I meet clients at their hotel, talk to them and ask them whether they're comfortable with me and do they want to confirm the job," she explains cheerfully. "If they do, I will call back to the agency and let them know that I have arrived safely and have collected the booking." Different agencies charge different booking fees—it can be S$200 for a two-hour minimum, sometimes a four-hour minimum, or S$100 an hour for a three-hour minimum. This fee is collected by the girl and returned to the agency, in exchange for which she may get a cut, depending on the agency's policy.

The real money, however, lies in what transpires beyond that minimum period, where the girls will provide what in the parlance of the Singapore escort trade is discreetly termed "extra services." Usually in the S$300 to S$500 range, the fee is privately negotiated between the gentleman and his companion. None of it goes back to the agency—the girl keeps it as her tip. "We are facilitating companionship, not marketing sex," is how one agency owner puts it. "What happens after the two or three or four hours of actual escorting are over, it's not for me to know. I don't know and I don't want to know." However, the agency makes money off this too, because the client has to "extend the booking" and he will then have to pay an extra S$100 or S$200 per the same hourly period. It is the girl's responsibility to collect this on behalf of the agency; the only money she's supposed to keep outright is her tip.

And the things they have to do, for that tip. Some escorting jobs don't involve sex at all. One lucky girl received a call at 7 a.m. to meet with a gentleman for breakfast. All she did was have breakfast with him, and at the end of the meal he tipped her S$500. Emily remembers going out on a lot of non-sex jobs where she collected several hundred dollars each time. "I show them around. They will ask me for Singaporean food and we'll go to Newton Circus or things like that. If they want seafood, I'll bring them to the East Coast, which is nice because we can stroll along the beach after dinner. If they want some nightlife, I'll take them to Brix, at the Hyatt.

"Sometimes, if the customer books me for several hours, like six hours, I'll take them to Victoria Street, to show them the open concept food courts and to teach them how to order. We don't always do the air-conditioned places. It all depends on what my customers like, rather than what I want."

Sometimes, the dates have unexpected outcomes, somewhat hilarious and at her expense. "One guy booked me to accompany him to a Malay wedding. He asked me to dress nicely. I presumed he would take a taxi because I was thinking it was a wedding lunch or reception or something. So I dressed in black and wore a jacket. It was so warm. But he made me walk from the escort agency office to Orchard MRT station, and take the train to Bedok and then take a feeder bus! Can you imagine? So many people were looking at me and I felt so stupid, wearing a jacket and taking a bus and then sitting at the HDB void deck [the open-sided ground floor of a housing project, built by the Singapore government's Housing Development Board]. There I was, having my lunch and pretending to be his girlfriend. He was a local Malay guy. A Malay wedding in an HDB void deck!"

"I meet all the weird customers," Emily sighs. "One time, this guy booked me for escorting and we met at Furama

33

Hotel, where he paid me the money and said, 'Okay, let's go.' I didn't know where he was taking me but I had already confirmed the job so I said okay. He took me to the Subordinate Courts! He said I had to pretend to be his girlfriend. His ex-girlfriend was there and he wanted me to be there just to provoke her. I was supposed to be his new girlfriend. I didn't have to say anything. I just sat through the entire hearing. I was terrified and embarrassed. I had never been to the courts before and here I was doing escorting in a courtroom! He tipped me S$200."

Even when there is no sex involved, Emily sometimes gets to role-play with clients who obviously have a rich fantasy life. Her favorite client, she says is an elderly gentleman. "Uncle Freddie. He's seventy or eighty years old. He would ask me to marry him and I would ask him for his bank account: 'Show me you can afford me first!' He would ask me to dance for him, seduce him. He would dance the Macarena! His dancing was stiff, like he was driving a car. But he always asks for me. No sex. I would give him a shower. He likes showers. And then I would talk to him. Tease and provoke him, 'Your dick is so *big*! Your dick grows so *long*!' He told me he takes Vitamin C with zinc and it makes his dick grow. It's fun! He would always book me on Saturdays and all I had to do was dance and keep him company. I like the fact that every Saturday is different, every Saturday would be a whole different story. It's quite fun, quite entertaining. And I don't have to have sex!"

But inevitably, Emily is frequently called for sex jobs, perhaps because she is highly adept at playing the requisite part. She thinks of herself as being paid to be an actress.

Fantasy sessions that accompany escorting are an elevated kind of play-acting. Granted, there's a pathos to it. It's Emily's only chance to be a star. "I seem to get all the funny calls, like having to pretend to be a doctor or a dentist. They would give me a gown and I would have to inspect them. One client had me check and then polish his genitals with Colgate. I had to polish his balls with an electric toothbrush and then put Colgate on his dick. He told me to make a humming sound while I was doing it, like a buzzing sound, which would excite him even more. He came! That was so funny. One guy even bought a doctor's outfit complete with stethoscope and asked me to put it on. That's extending the booking beyond the usual S$300 minimum, and then he would tip me S$600!"

Another time, Emily was asked to simulate necrophilia. "It was his fantasy to make love to a corpse—I was asked to play dead," she giggles. "This guy was a pathologist or a coroner, he worked in a mortuary, and he made me pretend to be dead. I was naked and lay there pretending to be dead while he checked my body parts. He was lifting my arms and snooping around between my legs. He got an erection and wanted to have sex with me. I was lying there, holding my breath and pretending to be dead, and then I got worried that he might not use a condom so I suddenly got up and gave him a condom and then lay down to pretend to be dead again!

"He cried out 'Hey, you can't get up, you're already dead!' I put the condom on my stomach for him to take, and lay down again. It was weird because I was not to move a muscle while he had sex with me. He liked it that way. Of course, I couldn't have an orgasm since I couldn't move! But he pays good money—he paid me S$1,000 for that! If I can get the big tips, I'll pretend to be anything. I've had customers who would pay me S$1,000 just to sleep next to them. You just sleep only, that's it. I can sleep anywhere, so it's not a problem. They will extend the booking just to watch me sleep! Probably when they're working they hardly have time to see their wives or girlfriends sleep."

Emily is under no illusions about escorting. She has a

husband who is ill and unable to work, and they have bills to pay. "If you think about the money, you can do anything, I believe that," she says firmly. "I can fake an orgasm, no problem."

What really turns Emily on these days, though, are the jobs that don't involve penetrative sex, that allow her to play out her own domination fantasies. "They pay me to whip them!" she enthuses. "I remember the first time I was sent out for a domination job. This was three years into my escorting career. This guy wanted to do an hour of massage and then after that we 'would discuss.' So, I went to the guy's home, confirmed the job and then the guy said he didn't want to have sex. I asked him what he wanted. He said he wanted domination. That was my first time. I didn't know what to do. I was shocked! People pay money to be whipped? I whipped him with a hanger. I didn't have anything else to whack him with, so I spanked him with the hanger.

"He said he wanted an additional service, a 'golden shower.' And I did it. I squatted over him and peed on his face. That's how he liked it. I even did a 'brown shower' once. This was for a European guy, a long time ago, at a hotel on Orchard Road. It was so late at night and I couldn't shit. He asked me drink black coffee and that helped. It took me so long to do it, though. I was in a bathtub with one leg on each side and his body underneath. I drank the coffee and jumped around a bit. I did it and he ate it. I shat into his mouth. It felt disgusting. I just think of the money and don't think of what I'm doing."

But there's one thing Emily has not yet done—the so-called "tiger show," which is the local term for a live sex show. "I have no problem with the idea of doing that," she says, "but I don't want anyone to tape it and circulate it. There have been guys who have videotaped girls and the girls end up crying. You never know what they do with the film. They might put it on the Internet."

We all have our sexual boundaries, explains Emily. Even for someone like her, whose comfort zone extends beyond that of most people. Emily becomes quite animated when she talks about her kinkier clients. "This Burmese guy had me tie him up and fill up the bathtub and then put his head in like I was going to drown him," she recalls. "I also did one guy in Bukit Timah who was bit of a pervert. He wanted to be a slave. He had me dress up in high heels and a short skirt and he would kiss my toes and lick my toes and then lick my four-inch high heels and then he wanted to use my high heels to squish his balls. And then, flip him upside down so he could eat his own sperm."

She leans back, gesticulates with her arms. "I had to poke the stiletto heel on his ass. I had to hold him, sit on a high stool and support his back with one leg while using the other leg to poke his anus—with my stiletto heel. So I'm pushing his back up with my thighs and legs, and he's lying with his legs up, and he masturbates and comes—into his own mouth. I did all this while smoking a cigarette!"

And when they want to be seriously violated, she'll do that too. "One guy wanted me to roll him with a rolling pin and then play with an egg blender on his privates. Then, he got out a big vibrator. He was tied up and he liked to be tortured with it, especially around his genitals. I also used candle wax but I wouldn't know if he was in pain or not because I gagged his mouth. I tied him up, whipped him, used paper clips to clip his balls, his dick, his nipples, everywhere. I would go back and tell the agency boss, and we would have a good laugh. If I couldn't laugh about it, I think I would have gone mad by now.

"I have issues from my childhood. My brother and sister would hang me upside down and cane me. If I didn't do the housework properly or if I didn't finish a task, they would cane me. My house has these ceiling hooks for hanging baby cots, and they hung a chain down, tied my legs, hung me upside down and caned me. I hated it so much. Now I cane people to take revenge!"

The violence, however, cuts both ways. She learned, rather traumatically, that she is not naturally submissive. "I can dominate but I cannot receive," she says. "There was one customer, Richard, he wanted to smack me on the backside. Just for five minutes, and he would give me S$500. But I couldn't take it. I was crying and crying. I got so upset not because of the pain but because of my childhood memories. That was the hardest job I've ever done.

"I have had customers who were somebody in their companies, heads of departments, and they would always like to be a slave. They wanted to make me coffee, massage me, bathe me. They even wanted me to humiliate them in public, which is something that I don't mind doing. I would scold them in public, tell them they're useless, things like that. Tell them they are my slave and must carry my shopping bags, scold them stupid and slow. I don't think of anything but the money, so it's kind of fun.

"I've also done strangling. I let the guy's head rest between my legs then I cross my legs together and apply pressure. I'll go out there with my colleague, Jasmine. We take turns and make sure the guy's still in one piece. If you know the tactic—how to hold somebody like that while applying pressure—you won't kill him. I don't have any kind of training in martial arts. You just have to focus. As long as you don't snap the neck, you will never kill a person.

"These jobs," she shrugs, "are about reenacting my childhood."

White Diamonds

Such girls, if they are gifted in their profession,
may make as much as US$180,000 a year in cities
like London, Los Angeles, New York, Chicago,
Paris, Hong Kong, Berlin, Tokyo, Singapore.
Of course they never pay tax, and usually they
save a significant amount, so within a few years
they return to join our wealthier classes.

—John Burdett, *Bangkok 8*

Marie, a blond-haired, blue-eyed Dutch girl, arrives in Singapore aboard Emirates flight 404 from Dubai with the intention of working for one month on the island. She needs to earn 700 euros to cover the plane ticket, anything extra will be pure profit. This is the standard way of working for a top-tier escort agency in Singapore, for girls fresh off the tarmac. Clients who specially request specific girls from overseas have to pay the airfare as well, but this is usually for the girls who regularly work the Asian circuit, who already have established reputations and sealed relationships.

Marie is new to Asia. But the continent holds a strange fascination for her. Marie's only previous taste of Asia was Japan, where she learned that her best asset was her blond hair. "It's better to be looked over than to be overlooked," was her motto, stolen from Mae West, while modeling in Tokyo. She had even appeared in a few Japanese music videos, always cast as the white chick of Japanese male fantasies.

Prior to Singapore, she had been based in Los Angeles, where she usually made US$1,000 for a two-hour job; US$250 for four hours was her absolute lowest, and that had happened only once, when she acquiesced to the discount price to placate a horny friend. Back in the West, she was not yet one of the top-tier girls; that echelon belonged to the New York call girls who made US$1,000 an hour, literally without leaving the house, and the porn stars who commanded US$2,000 an hour or more for the pleasure of their company.

But Marie knows how her bread is buttered. By the time she lands at Changi Airport, escorting is no longer a job to her, it's a whole way of life. It had taken her around the world. She's already lived in Australia, Greece, and South Africa. And so, for her to spend a month in Singapore, a country she's never been to, means the proverbial water off the duck's back. She's already given up her L.A. apartment on Overland Avenue in Culver City and is treating this stay as a transit stop, a busman's holiday, before heading back to Amsterdam for Christmas.

"My friend Eloise recommended me to the agency in Singapore, she'd worked for them before, and in fact she was working for them when we met as escorts in Amsterdam," Marie explains. "Eloise worked for them through their contact in London." Such an international presence these guys had, she thought, and was instantly impressed. She was lured like a moth to the flame, with thoughts of big money. The total population of Singapore currently stands at approximately 4.2 million, including 750,000 foreigners, and the gender ratio nationwide is 993 males per 1000 females. Marie read the 2003 Durex survey, in which the condom maker discovered that people around the world had sex an average of 127 times a year. Singapore finished last, at 96. Eastern Europeans (Hungarians, Bulgarians, Russians) were the most sexually active, at 150, while Americans scored a surprisingly low 118. Curiously, despite their humble status, 71 percent of Singaporeans claimed to be happy with their sex lives. Only 30 percent reported having had a one-night stand. What really made Marie laugh was reading that 39 percent admitted to using pornography to spice up their sex lives, despite the fact that it's illegal in Singapore. The survey also showed that a mere 18 percent admitted to paying for sex.

Somebody was fudging those numbers, surely, since prostitution *per se* is not illegal in Singapore. Working girls are confined to designated areas and have to be licensed; anyone caught openly soliciting can be arrested, the penalty being a fine of S$1,000 for the first offence and up to S$2,000 or a jail term of six months, or both, for subsequent offences. There are a lot of escort agencies, though, and girls often refer other girls to agencies, which is why the established companies always stay in business; the girls keep coming because the owners have their act together, they've established trust and rapport.

Trust and rapport. The entire industry relies on those two words.

The interesting thing about the escorting scene in Singapore is that there is no standard business model. Everyone sets their own rates. All agencies charge a booking fee with a minimum time limit, but some girls collect S$100 an hour for three hours, others S$200 for two hours, some even S$200 for four hours. The client pays the full amount if he falls short of the allotted time. It's also a 24-hour business, with a cancellation fee that automatically doubles after midnight; in most cases, a client who changes his mind or can't keep an appointment has to call to cancel the job and pay an extra S$20 if he's within the city limits, S$50 if he's living farther out.

The typical advice that agencies offer new clients is, as a local men's magazine once regurgitated, simply this: "Any fee for social escort services is simply for that person's time and companionship. Anything else that may take place is a matter of personal choice between consenting adults. If you are looking for a particular kind of companion, you should make it very clear when you book your date to avoid any embarrassing or potentially costly situation arising."

By the time she leaves Singapore, Marie has experienced the full measure of that. It's a funny country. There are at least ten shops selling sex toys, which are not illegal unlike in some American states. But oral sex, even among consenting adults, is actually illegal. In November 2003, a police officer was convicted under Section 377 of Singapore's Penal Code, for what was officially described as "carnal intercourse against the order of nature." He was found guilty of having received fellatio from a sixteen-year-old girl, whom he had been dating, and sentenced to one year in jail. (Sex with a girl under sixteen can lead to a five-year jail sentence and a S$10,000 fine.) Media interest sparked a public outcry, leading lawmakers to consider repeal.

Marie's biggest discovery was at the Heeren shopping mall on Orchard Road. She found a nipple-lightening cream for sale, in a Japanese beauty products store. Called Pink Nipples, it cost S$12.90, no doubt designed for Asian women hell-bent on Westernizing themselves. Marie stared at the tube for a good minute or so. It made her feel kind of special, like when she was in Japan. Some women in Asia clearly wanted to look more like her, with her blond hair and blue eyes, and there were surely men in Singapore willing to pay for the privilege of being with a blonde. She recalled a *Cosmopolitan* magazine survey showing that 66 percent of men fantasize about having sex with a woman of another race.

It actually doesn't matter to Marie whether the men are Asian or not. She is, after all, in the business of being a professional siren. The dictionary defines siren as "a seductively beautiful or charming woman, especially one who beguiles men." The only thing these men need to pique her interest is money to burn.

A week before returning to Holland, however, Marie experienced a customer who severely tested that paradigm.

The gentleman in question was an agency regular, a German stockbroker based in Singapore, living in Rochester Park and driving a BMW Z4 Roadster. After taking Marie to a pretentious French restaurant with *trompe l'oeil* murals, where he treated her to langoustine, artichoke salad, and *foie gras*, he asked her to indulge him his one unfulfilled fantasy: he wanted to have sex on the beach.

And so he drove her out to an East Coast beachfront popular with Singaporean lovers, where she ruined her dress on the sand. He was rough, but Marie kept telling herself to keep him past the minimum time, so that he would have to extend the booking and pay more. The booking fee was higher than usual, too; this agency charged more for white girls. Marie had been assured that her tip would be at least S$500.

On the drive back, however, he reneged on paying the full amount, disputing the length of the booking and refusing to pay for the extended time. An extra S$300 was all he offered.

He even tried to placate her by saying he would give her the missing S$200 if she'd just allow him to have sex with her again, in his car. She refused, and left.

But the next evening, to her amazement, he booked her again. This time, it was going to be a foursome. He was bringing a colleague and she was to meet them with another escort in tow. She went with Melissa, a young brunette from New Zealand.

The foursome went for drinks at Embargo, a fun chill-out lounge by the Marina Bay waterfront, but throughout the evening the German client ignored the two girls, talking corporate politics with his pal instead. Marie realized it was a set-up: this was his anal-retentive ego at work, using escorts as mere props, his trophy bimbos, a neat inversion of the local SPG phenomenon—"sarong party girls" refers to the dark, dusky local girls who troll Singapore's bars for rich white guys, and not merely for conversation.

"This was his way of flaunting his wealth," Marie recalls. "And when I told him we were leaving, he said, 'Alright,' and started taking out his wallet. We kind of stared at one another for a few seconds, like a two-gun Mexican standoff in a John Woo film, and then he started paying us. He counted the money out loud—'Here you are, fifty, fifty, that's one hundred. Another fifty, fifty, two hundred,' and so on, and he did the same with Melissa. I'd never been so humiliated in my life!"

He was, of course, making a point, openly telling the world that these girls were whores. That he could spend his money any way he liked. "I feel sad for him, that he had to prove his manhood that way," Marie concludes. Such are the occupational hazards of the profession. There are few ways around it, if one contemplates the big picture. Marie is just another foot soldier in a very complex war game. The same agency that hired her has a platoon of Hungarian girls, with names like Eva and Helga and Niki, already waiting in line and ready to be shipped out to Singapore. Some are already here, housed in a condominium where they've made new friends with girls from Australia, Bulgaria, Russia, the Ukraine; all of good Caucasian stock, with high cheekbones and hard Hollywood eyes.

While biding time between clients in Singapore, Marie read *Hotel Honolulu* by Paul Theroux, a novel with a prophetic opening line: "Nothing to me is so erotic as a hotel room, and therefore so penetrated with life and death." The interesting thing about escorting is that they work mostly in hotel rooms, and most of them luxurious five-star suites. In some ways, this means they are spared the tawdry tales of the sex business's lower rungs. Comedy is, of course, sometimes rife in that side of things, like the story about a randy Aussie named Geoff who was having the time of his life with a slip of a Thai girl in Bangkok. During sex she kept shouting, "Jep! Jep!" He thought he was in heaven. When had a girl ever screamed out his name while they were having sex? However, the next day, someone told him that "Jep!" in Thai means "Painful!"

Marie recalls one incident that was painful, in an existentialist kind of way. She was booked in to meet a gentleman in his hotel suite but when the door opened, she was confronted with a vision out of *La Cage Aux Folles*. The client was a cross-dresser. "When he opened the door, I wanted to laugh. He was wearing make-up and a red dress and red high-heel shoes and stockings. And a red scarf. He was all decked out in red! He used this very strong perfume too, *White Diamonds*, from Elizabeth Taylor. That's why I remember it. It was so strong, I kept wanting to sneeze!

"So anyway, he asked me to take off my clothes. And he fucked me, like that. He fucked me wearing those clothes and those high heel shoes. He was on top of me, wearing all that make-up, very strong make-up, fake eyelashes, and he was wearing a wig. He came very quickly, with a condom. I asked him if he was comfortable in those clothes, and he said, 'Yes, I want to wear this.' He removed his stockings, and then he fucked me. That was his fantasy. Sometimes they fantasize about girls fucking another girl, but this guy, he wanted to *be* the girl."

He paid Marie S$500 extra, on top of the booking fee. She sighs. What's a girl to do to earn a little money? She related the story to the madam back at the agency, who laughed out loud. Years ago, when the madam herself was an escort, she had gone to a hotel room and found a middle-aged English gent waiting. The man did not want sex with her at all.

"She told me that the guy wanted her to do make-up for him," Marie explains, "and when she said she didn't have any make-up with her, the man just giggled and said not to worry. He produced a make-up case, and asked her to use it. This guy actually traveled with a make-up case!" So she did his make-up, dolling him up to look like the most glamorous transsexual ever. He already had a wig on and was dressed in a satin evening gown, every bit the woman of his dreams. "And when it was done, he had her watch while he looked at himself in the mirror and masturbated to his own image."

When asked by the madam whether his wife was aware of his curious predilection, he replied, "No, she wouldn't understand." None of his four children knew either. It was that well-kept a secret, hidden from his own family. When he was young, the man explained, he had a very dominant mother and his only siblings were three sisters. He would marvel when they did their make-up and hair and got dressed to go out for the evening. He had osmosized his childhood ambience, obviously. When he finally had the means, he paid for escorts to help him enact his fantasy.

Singapore's geographical position makes it a perfect place for escorts to work. The fact that many major companies have their regional head offices here means a steady influx of business visitors, who always comprise the main market for high-end escorts. Even in a lean year like 2003, the visitor arrivals were up; by November 2003, the total number of visitors to Singapore was 5.4 million, not quite the 6 million mark the Singapore Tourism Board had hoped for but it was a 7.9 percent increase over the number for the previous November. Not bad, given the SARS crisis back in March, which had sent the travel industry into free fall.

The escort agencies were all affected by the SARS slump, but in general the girls were inoculated from the malaise that affected the general public. So what if unemployment in Singapore stood at a record high of 5.9 percent, thanks to the downward spiral of the 1997 Asian economic crisis? Girls like Marie with good connections could work anywhere, and she had the stamps in her passport to prove it.

Newly affluent, emerging economies were always fertile training grounds for escorts. Places like Singapore bring together people from everywhere, and Marie sees herself as promoting international relations. There were two best friends, for instance, one Australian and one Italian, who booked Marie one night for a torrid threesome, at an Orchard Road hotel. Earlier that evening, she'd felt quite regal at dinner with the two men, looking very hot in her low-cut, red halter dress that held the promise of late-night excitement. The idea came from a DeBeers diamond ad, in which a glamour model wore a dress much like hers. "The suggestion," interpreted the eminent British fashion editor Prudence Glynn in her 1982 book *Skin to Skin: Eroticism in Dress*, "is that if you buy the girl a very expensive piece of jewelry, she will grant you certain privileges."

Marie, with her long blond hair and enviably slim, five-foot-nine frame, had the look commensurate with those privileges and now that she had arrived, she wasn't going to compromise anything. Her dress wasn't new, but it was a classic Azzedine Alaia she'd procured in London, a throwback to the more moneyed years of the 1980s. Not for her the red sari that Bollywood star Kareena Kapoor, granddaughter of the great Raj Kapoor and star of Deepa Mehta's *River Moon*, wore when she played a typical Indian sex worker in *Chemeli*, a film made for 30 million rupees (S$1.13 million). Kapoor's sari had cost only 400 rupees. That kind of authenticity only served to instill the idea that sex workers had to look cheap.

That's why Marie spared no expense to perfect her arsenal of beauty weapons. The lipstick, lip gloss, lip brush, and lipliner pencils. She spent a fortune on facials, on mascara and moisturizers. And she never left home without her Astroglide. "I prefer to have guys who can have fun," she says. "Some girls don't like that, they think it's too much work and it gets too personal. They do see it as work. But that's because they're not really interested in them as people. Mind you, people always tell me I'm 'interesting' and by that I think they mean I talk a lot. I was on the debate team in school. It's not always an asset, though, not when it's compared to Western values here. I mean, I think the local, traditional Chinese in Singapore don't like the likes of me.

I'm too forward and I intimidate them."

Her constant challenge, she says, lies in perfecting her social skills. "The way it works is to see how you do the first one or two hours, to get a fix on the body language, which can sometimes make me a bit nervous. It takes an effort to form different personas to survive in this job. You'll go meet someone and there's the initial twenty minutes of awkwardness. But I usually find a way to get them to like me. I'm very sociable, I'm a people person. Getting dinner is a bonus. And it helps that I like to drink Champagne.

"I'm also a night person, I like to stay out late. Usually, after dinner, you might go to a bar or go sing karaoke somewhere. Sometimes the guy I'm with will meet another guy and we'll meet up with another girl so there's four of us. I usually get to bed at around 3 a.m. or 4 a.m., anyway. One time, I went back to this guy's room and he passed out drunk. The next morning, he said he couldn't remember a thing. We never had sex or did anything. Another time, a guy gave me a back massage and a foot massage. That was so great! I like the traveling, too. This job is my way of maximizing the limited time I have in life."

Marie takes serious umbrage at the idea that she can be thought of as a prostitute. "There are people you wouldn't call prostitutes but they're called personal assistants. The kind that types letters and takes dictation and they'll fuck half the office anyway." But she admits that it's a far more subtle game, and so "there's a thrill to it, though it's not the same as doing armed robbery or intentionally speeding on the freeway. It's the whole thing of, 'Hmm, I wonder if I can get away with this.'"

Escorting, in her final analysis, "is necessary in society. Marriages get boring and people need people. There are some guys who have a lot of money or power or position but they often don't meet the right people." Men, she believes, are not always oversexed animals and her work fills a vital social need. "Businessmen who travel a lot get lonely, they like to have dinner with someone and have someone to talk to. There are those who are married, and all they do is talk to me about their wives!"

Should a client take a shine to her, dangerously falling in love, Marie recalls the words of Heidi Fleiss, from her book, *Pandering*, about her life as America's most notorious madam: "When a guy tells you how much he loves you, and wants to have babies with you, he means I love having sex with you for free. Free meaning no obligations. Men will promise the world to get laid. When a guy and a girl are about to have sex, a guy will promise her anything under the sun. As soon as he cums, he's like, 'Get the fuck out! I don't know who you are. I've never seen you before in my life.'"

"I would be horrified," Marie insists, "if one of the guys wanted to marry me or something." Her eyes are suddenly wide. A slightly defensive, sudden choke catches in her throat. "It'll never happened to me."

Asian Affairs

> They were both across the borderland of
> their youth, traveling with visas on the verge
> of expiration, imperiled by the pending truth
> of their trespasses.
>
> —Steve Erickson, *Days Between Stations*

Amelia's dark green eyes are pretty and penetrating, offering the insouciant look of someone who has deftly steered across some desperate straits, visited the dangerous places of the heart. Very been-there, done-that.

Until three years ago, though, she had never done Singapore.

"I thought Singapore was quite repressed, sexually," admits Amelia. "I didn't think there were any legal brothels here." Back in her native Australia, some states permit a girl to work as an escort but not as an "in-house" girl, whereas in other states the reverse is true. Some of the more progressive cities, like Sydney and Melbourne, are similar to Singapore, where you can actually do both.

Maybe that's why she likes the Singapore scene, having done both herself back home.

Amelia grew up in the Barossa Valley, where the grapes billow gently on the vines. She went to Catholic school in Adelaide and then on to university in Sydney. Many a lad harbored a secret crush on this tall, slender brunette with the chiseled cheekbones, headed for stardom via the fashion magazines. There she was, all tanned and aglow in a bikini, on exotic islands like Menorca and Stromboli. Striding down the catwalk in Paris and Milan. Even appearing on an MTV-style talk show about the sex-and-drugs, bad-girl lifestyles of next-generation supermodels. She totally looked the part: all svelte and sassy, a fuck-me Elizabeth Hurley-type of girlie, sans the posh Pommie accent. She was all of nineteen at the time, the world her succulent oyster.

But the years flew by and it was back to the billabong. Amelia came home. No more melatonin, no more binges on meth and coke. And, given her freeform lifestyle, no more money either. Europe had proved expensive, even with her modeling wages; she's not sure even today just where the money went, except that it funded the whims and fancies of her carefree youth. To be sure, though, she didn't miss the spotlight. Not when she could now openly display a mermaid tattoo on her right forearm and a silver stud on her tongue, the new tribal markings for her new career.

"I saw an advert in a newspaper, claiming that you could make up to A$2,000 a week," she remembers, sipping Tiger Beer in Holland Village. And looking a tad misty-eyed, though it might have been the beer. "So I went in for an interview. And it was in-house, a brothel. That's when they told me it was in the sex industry, and they wouldn't let me go. They said, 'Why don't you stay here this afternoon and you'll go home with A$400."

"And that's what I did," she says. "That's how they hook you. They showed me around, told me what to do in the rooms. I was twenty-four, still at uni, and my whole first year was spent paying for my books and my studies and finishing my degree. Nobody knew for quite a long time."

Then, the talk started. Her car had been spotted near the house. "I started to be known in various social circles and it started to get difficult," she admits. "Also, some of the girls were very open about what they did, so if you were seen with them you tend to get labeled as the same thing. People I'd either confided in or told became annoying. So I had to relieve myself of that social atmosphere when I stopped working, to clear my name again."

"I think my parents were clever enough to figure it out, since I ended up buying a really nice car and I hadn't even finished uni yet," she recalls. "I had set up a whole scenario about where I was going at night and that I had my own job and I'd come home with bogus stories about what happened at work. It was quite taxing, actually, to continue a double life in that way."

Amelia left the in-house life for good and switched to escorting—supposedly a more discreet and somewhat safer choice. "I wouldn't ever go back to what I was doing before," she insists. "Your establishment owns you, at the time, but then again you're sort of freelancing amongst that and so you put pressure on yourself, fighting for the clients. And have them return to you, you know, because some get you bonuses, if they return to you." The repeat customers elevated her bank balance, but the ploy backfired somewhat, since all it did was make Amelia's own family even more suspicious. They were beginning to wonder how she suddenly made so much money, even more than when she was modeling, and she once let slip that she was already thinking of buying her first house.

Four years later, in 2003, Amelia owned two houses. Now a twenty-eight-year-old single mother with a ten-year-old son (she had the boy when she was eighteen and never married), she has only one burning ambition left in life: to write a book called *The Escort's Way*, a self-help tome for girls like her. She thinks she can be an example to others. That's why she named herself Amelia, after the Joni Mitchell song. "*I was driving across the burning desert when I spotted six jet planes, leaving six white vapor trails across the bleak terrain.*" She'd cased her terrain well, stampeded the bleakness out with a fiery might. And it all started by getting the hell out of Australia.

"Your market there is Australian people," she shudders, "and they are only willing to pay very minimum amounts to get their rocks off and go home. Because of the culture, or the lack of it, you might have worked six or eight hours a day and you may have gotten six clients in the eight hours." She agrees with the perception a lot of Australian girls have of their men; the last of the great romantics, fair dinkum being a shag and a root, mate. Even Germaine Greer, arguably Australia's most famous female writer, had controversially declared that Australians were "too relaxed to give a damn," a view which prompted some clarification from the Prime Minister himself. "What she basically says," said the unflappable, honorable John Howard, "is that the average Australian is too stupid to think about anything that's the least bit philosophical or important."

Amelia is no average Australian, she learned philosophy the hard way, right there in the cathouse.

"There would sometimes be periods of time where you wouldn't be working for a couple of hours at all," she notes. "That was probably the most painful time, working in-house, because you would be in your little uniforms and sitting on couches with all the other girls and you weren't allowed to watch TV, you weren't allowed to have any music, you're sort of looking at each other and looking at the floor. Trying to kill time. That's when it becomes very obvious to you why you are there."

Asia is more lucrative, she decided, and left. She flew to Singapore, where she modeled for the agencies but escorted on the side. She couldn't fail with her striking good looks, and of course the men loved her. She knew how to walk the walk and talk the talk. Charm a client over dinner, learn to be a good listener, and a good lover too. Exude worldly aura, glow incandescently, gleam with sophistication. Not like those tacky chicks at Orchard Towers, hawking their wares in public for the redneck American sailors.

Amelia went there one night just to check out the scene but left in disgust. She saw a blond Polish girl, who called herself Sonja, openly propositioning a guy in the open. "Two hunnred fifty dollar, you vant?!! "Now?!!" shrieked Sonja. No wonder the guy backed away. How vulgar. Sluts like Sonja should stay in Warsaw and drown in vodka piss, thought Amelia.

Of course, the Sonjas of the world proliferate the globe like cockroaches, in numbers far greater than more refined escorts like Amelia. To make it as an escort takes far greater skill than hawking your wares openly in Orchard Towers, though often the deck is stacked against you, as Amelia discovered on a brief and unsuccessful foray to Hong Kong.

"You can come to Singapore with nothing, stay in a really cheap hotel, and start making money straight away," states Amelia. "I went to Hong Kong for two weeks, but I didn't work there when I found out what it was like. It's a whole different market. The agents tell you to bring in US$3,000 and only then will they have you on the books. Well, I didn't have US$3,000, so they said, 'You can't work for us.' In Hong Kong, even though there is an agency, you don't go and drop in your money every day like you do here in Singapore. So probably, over seven days, you will be carrying about US$3,000. But the agency wants that as a deposit! That's how it works. You've got to have the money upfront, to give to them, for them to give you the work. You've got to have the money to start."

Here in Singapore, she can do dinner and karaoke and if nothing's happened after the minimum time of three or four hours, she can say, "Nice to meet you, goodbye." No fanfare and no fuss, unless he has heaps of cash and makes her an offer she can't refuse. Either way, there's no monetary outlay on her part; she returns the booking fee to the agency and keeps the rest, assuming there's any. If there's no sex, some agencies will actually split the booking fee with the girl, some as much as fifty-fifty.

Amelia still remembers her first job as an escort, when she was back in Australia. Perhaps presciently, the client was Asian. "I met a guy who used to play the casinos and he used to entertain the Asian junkets that would come, all those high-rollers, and that's how I got into escorting. My first escorting job was actually with a guy and his girlfriend—a threesome! The girl wanted to be with another girl and the guy obviously found me suitable, especially with my background. But his girlfriend was a bit conservative, and I was supposed to be full of all this experience, of the sex industry, and so she was very intimidated by me. They actually ended up arguing, and I went home."

"No sex!" Amelia laughs at the memory, with a droll fondness. "We went out to dinner and then went up to the room, and then she was upset with me. I felt uncomfortable and I knew that she was uncomfortable. She was an Australian girl and he was an Asian guy. Maybe in the experience of his culture, it was quite normal but obviously it wasn't for her, so it didn't work out."

That baptismal trial, despite its anti-climactic ending, endeared Amelia to Asia. "The Asian market is very different from anywhere in the world," she observes, almost admiringly. "In a cultural way. Men in Asia are used to having mistresses and girlfriends. They are willing to spend money on that kind of entertainment. They are willing to spend more and so the work is less cut-and-dry physical. Here they want to do karaoke, they want to go out, they want you to go on holiday with them. It's much more appealing to work here."

"And I've come to learn," Amelia adds, "that there are three kinds of Asian clients. One is where they have a lot of guilt associated with being there in the first place, and they're very worried about someone seeing them or losing face," she says. "They don't talk. They just have sex and then they leave. And then you have the second level, where they have to go to certain parts of Asia to be seen with me. Being seen with me becomes an issue. They will want to have dinner and they will want talk. They enjoy intelligent conversation, finding out about you and stuff like that. It's great.

"The third one is the type who falls in love, you know, the type that wants a girlfriend. Most of the time, I've had the type who falls in love." She laughs shyly, reaches into her jeans pocket, digs out her cigarette case and pulls out a Marlboro Light. "Yeah. I think, you know, because I'm working, I'm fascinated by their conversations. And they like that. Everything is very attentive. Their experience of being with me is about having very attentive moments with them. And so, that is where feelings break out. They fall in love with the concept of me being very good listener and a good companion, as opposed to their girlfriend who might nag them all the time."

"It gets you into trouble sometimes," she laughs nervously. "I've just become more and more aware of those three levels of guys. I know what's going on within the first hour. I can tell which kind they are. I've had all three. The ones who fall in love tend to give you a lot more gifts. But after a short period of time, they don't feel they should be paying you anymore. You become a 'girlfriend' and they see you in that way. And so they take you out to dinner and they take you around the world. But the actual financial tab, they want to stop that happening.

"And that's not where I'm at. That's how I get into a lot of trouble."

The eventual problem isn't really about separating love from sex. "I think that if you start seeing it as just sex, you don't have to separate it at all," she quips matter-of-factly. The real tough one is how to reject the client emotionally without losing his patronage. After all, you still need his money. The worst thing you can do, in Amelia's opinion, is to bruise his ego with the classic kiss-off: "Sorry, but I can't love you back."

"You'd be stupid to do that! An inexperienced escort will do that," she says. "The way you have to do it is, it has to be made a financial situation again. It's more about money. It is. You are there for a purpose. You are flattered by their feelings for you, but you have to deal with the issues by reminding them that financially, you are not going to continue being their girlfriend in life."

Without losing them as clients? "Exactly. I've had many experiences, with many different mentalities. You end up finding out who they really are, you get to the core of the person real fast. You find out if they're really neurotic, you know, from the way they expect you to like them back the way they like you. They have all these issues, which shouldn't be part of the scenario."

"It's a continual problem," Amelia sighs. She has never fallen for a client. "No. I have a lot of warm feelings for a lot of my clients. But there is always a line. I can love them for the people that they are, but no, there is a natural ceiling."

That's perhaps the main drawback of escorting: the close interpersonal contact where personalities get drawn out through intimate tête-à-tête, where the essence of a man can be found in the things he says, be it about his life or his wife. In the immortal words of Axelle Guerin, an escort who testified for Margaret MacDonald, the British madam convicted in September 2003 of running a high-class sex ring in Paris, "I knew I would be expected to sleep with men. They wouldn't pay me that much money just to look into my eyes."

In lower-level forms of sex work, the art of looking into a lover's eyes might well be the only kind of non-sex exchange. When men rave about brothels, they're not exactly extolling the virtues of conversation. At a famous whorehouse like Atlantis, located forty minutes' drive outside Frankfurt, Germany, a client can choose from an array of girls parading around in the nude, clad only in heels. Sex costs 50 euros per half-hour. In Singapore, a man can choose a Thai girl for just S$40 in one of the legal brothels in Geylang, or find himself serviced for less by a compliant *peidu mama* (literally, a "study mother"), a mainland Chinese woman working, usually in a massage parlor, to support her young children studying in Singapore. One can even get a S$20 quickie with an older woman in the Keong Saik Road area of Chinatown or in Little India.

V.J. Seidler, in his 1989 book *Rediscovering Masculinity: Reason, Language and Sexuality*, concludes that "getting off" with a woman is a man's way of "affirming self-esteem and masculine identity," rooted actually in a fear of vulnerability and rejection. "It is as if we want to deny the link between sexuality and vulnerability," he argues. "As men we often have sex without vulnerability, for when we are vulnerable we fear that we can be rejected...so it is that control becomes a crucial issue, because in controlling our partners we minimize the risk of rejection."

But the sword cuts both ways, and a seasoned escort like Amelia will readily disclose that control is the most critical issue in her profession. Money is certainly the most obvious means of control, but when she has to deal at close quarters with men made of such means, she learns how to use her body as a bargaining chip. There are boundaries she has drawn for herself, for instance, with which she plays the game. For one thing, she does not consent to anal sex. "It's a personal thing for me, to be invaded in those areas," she explains. "Also, I would never tell my clients that I like a position because they will keep trying to get me to be in that position. To put myself in a situation where I may come. So even if they ask me, I'll say something else other than what I really like. When it comes to sex, I'm not even there at work. I'm just thinking about him coming, as soon as possible. For three hours, it's about entertaining him and meeting someone and learning about someone, but when it comes to being in bed, that's when it's about time and you have to do what you have to do to get him to finish."

"Being on top is actually my favorite position," Amelia confides. "Physically, your clitoris is in the way, so you can actually come. I wouldn't want to be on top of a client who knows I like that position, because he will keep wanting me to come, but yes, I orgasm better in that position. I think that's pretty normal for most women. Men don't really understand women in that way. Have you heard of many women coming in missionary? Are you sure they're telling you the truth? I don't think men ever know if a woman's faking it.

"The strangest thing I've had to do was when I was here in Singapore the last time. There are these three steps that you sort of follow when it comes to sex, but when you have a man who is not following the normal steps..." Amelia halts, lights another cigarette, inhales the nonplussed moment. "This guy was just *not* normal," she whispers. "He could get it up but he was just not going to come. So he wanted me to strap on a dildo and give it to him up the arse."

She pauses again. "It was quite an experience. It made me think, he's a heterosexual guy and seems normal on the outside, but when it comes down to sex, well...I don't know. What would a heterosexual man get from being penetrated that way? I did it. And the whole time, I was in shock. It was the only way that he could come."

Meaning that the guy ejaculated as Amelia sodomized him. That may not be a big head trip for some girls, like porn stars for whom anal sex and double-penetration are par for the course, but it was for Amelia. It went beyond her boundaries of acceptable behavior, and she freaked out. "Was he really heterosexual with me? He wasn't interested in my body at all. That was the only way he could get off. So I'm like, what is that?!! Is that heterosexual? Is that homosexual? Is that a heterosexual who is actually homosexual? I don't think he is either of those!"

Whatever, Amelia ended up having a fight with the agency owner, for not charging more. "You have to pay me double!" she screamed. "This is not normal sex!" The client had paid her S$2,000, but the owner kept S$800 so she ended up with only S$1,200. Plus a bunch of conflicted emotions.

Amelia stubs out her cigarette, not fully smoked, ash and flame spewing sideways. "I'd never even worn a strap-on in my life! Some people want to be entertained in ways that are an abnormality! My own life is *so* normal!"

Mentally, she plummeted back to her Sydney in-house days, haunted by her very own line: "That's when it becomes very obvious to you why you were there." Awestruck again by the same realization, that she was being paid to be a performing seal. Indeed, Amelia, perhaps more than most young women of her age and ambition, has had lots of occasions to decide just what sort of sex worker she is. "Well, I think a man would probably call an escort a prostitute," she argues. "But a woman can go out on dates where you end up in a sexual relationship. And then they're moving in with them and taking care of some of the bills, especially in this day and age where two incomes are normal, so it's still about a payoff, you know.

"You might be in love with this person but you have to maintain a sexual relationship and a personal relationship with that person, so that financially you're secure. So, I think there are different ways of looking at it." Her thoughts on the matter, she now says, came to true focus during her stay in Asia, "where it's okay to be someone's companion for a couple of hours. You get paid to have dinner and talk to the person, make him feel special, and then you have sex. And I believe that from a client's point of view, subconsciously, that it's the whole three hours for the sex, that's what he's buying into as soon as he pays me.

"What makes him make that phone call to the agency to book me is the last hour. But actually, it's the first three hours that he's really craving. That's what he wants and that's what makes an escort. Whereas a prostitute services people who just want to get their rocks off and go home. You're paid to just be physically involved with that person. I like escorting better, because I'm interested in people. In talking to them and learning about their concepts of life or what's reflective of their psychology as people. That fulfills a need in me. It's far more fascinating to me, to be an escort and go through those subtleties, rather than to be just used as a physical object."

However, there is now a major subtlety at work in her own life, a metaphysical quandary she hadn't anticipated. "For me, if you're financially independent as a woman, it's hard to fall in love, to be wanting to be cared for by a man. You don't need that anymore. And so that's one of the big issues for me. I want to fall in love with someone but I'm so independent and I'm so financially able, whether I'm working in this industry or not, the mentality is so ingrained that I can do it on my own.

"I think Singaporean women still want to marry to be looked after. But for me, it's not an issue. Even if I meet someone who is amazing, I don't need to compromise my natural state to be with him. Whereas a lot of other women will."

That, she's quick to admit, makes for a very problematic private life. Amelia did meet someone recently and they hit it off, so she's been thinking about this sort of thing a great deal. "I think if you're working, it screws up your private relationships," she says. "Because that's one major issue— you don't need a man for anything. When I first started working, I was compromising a lot more, because I saw my partner as someone whom I had to please. It's very natural for me to please a man—that's what I do on a natural basis, with my clients—and so, I have to feel like I'm in control in the private relationships that I have. Because I won't stand for this and I won't stand for that. It has to do with my need to be more dominant, because my needs have to be met. I feel sorry for whoever's my boyfriend."

Sex, for Amelia, has actually become a somewhat deadening experience. "Because it's a job, I desensitize myself down there and just not feel anything," she admits. "And so, when it became more important in my private life to be enjoying myself in the moment, it became an issue for me. What's wrong with me? Why can't I come?!! It's something that takes a lot of time and a lot of energy, and the right partner, to bring it around."

Amelia plans to have enough money to quit the business in six months. "But it's a whole different ball game now. I'm not interested in clothes or material things. I'm interested in going back to school, having enough money to finish school, those are the most important things to me. Everybody has to go through the process. You learn that you can't just get whatever you want, whenever you want. You learn to get more serious about what you're doing to yourself and what you're getting in return."

Amelia knows that when she finally writes *The Escort's Way*, she will offer one profound lesson to any girl brave or foolish enough to follow her footsteps. "The saddest thing about this industry is that you get used to so much money and how easy it is to obtain it. So you tend to spend it. If you don't have a level head or a goal in mind, then you're continuing a vicious cycle where you're working and spending, working and spending. That's how it was for me when I started. I could buy clothes. I could buy my car. I can buy this, this, this. And then, I would be down to my last ten dollars and I would have to go back to work."

"When you're starting out, you just don't understand that," she says quietly. "Not for a good long time."

PART TWO

Different Strokes

Her Heart Will Go On

"My mom once told me that every girl
wonders inside if she could be, you know,
a whore," Jackie says as she exhales smoke.
"She said when I came to Tokyo, this would
be my chance to find out."

—Karl Taro Greenfeld, *Speed Tribes*

Jennifer, a *mamasan* at a successful Singapore karaoke bar,
lights another cigarette, orders another beer for herself,
and plunks the newspaper down on the bar counter. The
news from Taiwan, she admits, bothers her. How could some
people be so stupid, so narrow-minded, especially in this day
and age?

She is reacting to the controversy that had recently erupted
in Taipei, over the Christmas holidays. Twenty-five-year-old
Kao Ching-Hui had been crowned Miss Taiwan on
December 28, 2003, but only after tearfully denying

allegations that she had once worked as a bar hostess—a contest no-no because of the profession's links to prostitution.

Yes, Ms Kao admitted, the bar was run by her sister, but she was not employed as a hostess, "just a cashier and never served wine to clients." Lining the ridiculous with the sublime was the fact that Kao was actually the first runner-up at the pageant held back in July. She had now been conferred the crown because the winner, one Liu An-Nan, had to be replaced—because she had gone into hiding to evade loan sharks! Liu had amassed debts of some NT$40 million, and the contest organizers stripped her of her title and gave it to Kao.

Chinese culture, not much given to overt sexual display, actually has a nickname for girls in hostess bars: *san pei* ("three services"), because they're hired to perform in the presence of men the three basic services—drinking, singing, and dining. The "dining" part, however, suggests something more akin to escorting, since escorts are always inclined towards dining with their clients. It lends to them the mystical aura of the Japanese *geisha*, a class of women whose place in society is to function solely as entertainers to men.

But this new Miss Taiwan insisted she was no *geisha*. "I did not drink with the patrons, and I only worked as an accountant," Kao told the *Taipei Times*. "Plus, this is my sister we're talking about, and she wouldn't have let me work as a bar girl." However, Kao's sister's ex-boyfriend, Chang Tso-wu, alleged that Kao did indeed work as a bar girl and drank with the bar's patrons. "Three years ago, my ex-girlfriend opened a bar," Chang was quoted. "Kao Ching-hui cannot drink much but she is pretty and gentle, and the patrons liked her. She was the star of the bar."

A star she had become indeed; photos of her wearing her pearl crown and red Miss Taiwan sash were posted all over the Internet. "She looks very pretty, a bit like Gong Li," Singapore *mamasan* Jennifer says. "I would love to have hired her here."

"Here" is 7,000 square feet of party space, packaged as a karaoke bar—or KTV bar, as karaoke bars are more popularly known in Singapore. Jennifer's KTV bar is a temple of sleek black-and-chrome splendor, a semi-circular array of private rooms adorning one side and a large lounge area and dance floor on the other. Come 8 p.m. every evening, groups of girls congregate in disparate cliques, lounging in feline repose on the black leather couches, smoking cigarettes, waiting for the men to arrive.

Jennifer is their *mamasan*, the lady who rules the roost.

There are thirty-two girls working there: fifteen Singaporeans, ten Chinese nationals, and seven Vietnamese. The club also has a *papasan*, a man whose jobs is to mingle with the guests, do some nudging and winking *mano a mano*, and generally keep a keen eye on the girls from mainland China. Most *papasan* are Mandarin speakers, and they usually earn a basic monthly salary of S$1,800 to S$2,000 plus tips (up to S$500 from each room) as well as commission on the booze consumed.

Additionally, Jennifer has an assistant *mamasan*, Lena, and they play good cop/bad cop with the staff. Jenny does the scolding, Lena the soothing, and this dynamic duo with their attitude/lassitude combo somehow keeps the ship on an even keel. In this floating world, *mamasan*s are both loved and feared. Even in Singapore, a socially conservative country, there have been quite a few *mamasan* who have elevated themselves to positions of social stature, having transcended the "cabaret girl" pariah class.

The most legendary of the Singapore *mamasan* is Mona Koh, the famous *mamasan* of the Lido Palace nightclub who survived an assassination attempt in 1994. An unknown gunman shot her twice as she was leaving an East Coast shopping mall. One bullet entered her face, the other her spine. The former was removed but the other remained lodged, causing her to be paralyzed from the waist down. Even so, wheelchair-bound at age fifty-five, she continued working as a *mamasan* and, more recently, expanded her sideline food business in Tiong Bahru, with plans for new restaurants in Shanghai, China.

And then there's Tysha De Morris, 30, an Australian who worked as a *mamasan* in Singapore for over a decade before recruiting ten *mamasan* and thirty hostesses to form a new agency in 2003, supplying talent to the clubs. Generally, a good *mamasan* earns S$3,000 a month, though a really excellent one can make up to S$30,000. However, *caveat emptor*, because the taxman doth cometh: Irene Su, forty-eight years old, made history on January 13, 2004, when she became the first *mamasan* to be charged with tax evasion in Singapore. Her photo appeared in *The Straits Times* along with the report that she admitted failing to declare S$325,213 in booking commissions for two years and was therefore liable for S$58,483 in taxes.

Her real name, Lee Phui Fan, was publicly revealed, as was her place of employment: the Tiananmen KTV and Lounge on Havelock Road, where she was the top earner with more than twenty girls under her wing. Fined S$2,000 after pleading guilty, she was also ordered to pay S$116,967.20, twice the tax undercharged but no doubt preferable to three years in jail.

Still, this Irene Su had cut a fashionable figure in the courtroom, clad in a pink shirt, black slacks and stylish, purple-hued sunglasses. The old image of a loud-mouthed, hard-drinking floozy all gussied up in big hair and flashy clothes no longer applies. Today's *mamasan* wear body-hugging, branded tops matched by suede skirts. They carry monogrammed Louis Vuitton clutch bags, which they'll casually fling into their Lexus SUVs. Sporty cars, not the lumbering Mercedes-Benzes of past epochs, are their status symbols. And they don't play mahjong anymore, preferring to spend their leisure time procuring jewelry and watches at the likes of Bulgari and Chopard. Alexis Bittar earrings, Kleinberg Sherrill silk satin bags—things once unheard of, now coveted. They now own the same kinds of mad-money accessories of the jet-setting, ladies-who-lunch *tai-tai*, with platinum credit cards to burn.

Not yet a Mona Koh, perhaps thankfully, *mamasan* Jennifer is nonetheless quite the class act. At the tender age of twenty-eight (virtually unheard of for a *mamasan*) the ethnic Malay woman (Jennifer, of course, is only her work name) is a single mother who leaves her young son in the care of her parents when she's commanding her little slice of estrogen heaven. Her fleet of thirty-two girls, however, is not the only proof of her ascendancy; she also has three sugar daddies wrapped around her pert pinky. All three men are married, so she only sees them in the daytime, and none of them know of one another. Through this high-wire act of emotional subterfuge, her S$400-a-month cellphone bills are paid for her, as well as some of her credit card payments. One of her sugar daddies is even helping her repay the loans that had forced her into the business in the first place.

"I was in very deep trouble, up to S$50,000 in debt," Jennifer recalls. Her ex-husband was a compulsive gambler, and what started out as co-dependency resulted in acrimony and divorce. "I started off as a 'girl,' a hostess, at a KTV place in Upper Serangoon. A very small place, only four rooms. After that I moved to a bigger KTV bar on Prinsep Street, as an assistant *mamasan*, and then I moved up to being a *mamasan* myself at a KTV bar with twenty-five rooms, a Japanese lounge. I finally came here when this place opened. I interviewed for it. I think I got the job based on my experience."

She looks around as the men, mostly business executive

types, start sauntering in. "I like this place better, because we have a better clientele, a mix of Chinese, Indians, and Caucasians." She likes the looser, less predictable atmosphere. At Japanese bars, for instance, the girls have to put up with kinky Japanese tastes. At the lounge she'd last worked at, a guy insisted on having her watch while another girl performed oral sex on him. ("The guy just wanted me to sit there and watch. I was like, 'Oh my God!'") Another guy made her strip down to her G-string and then he asked her to take his shirt off and wear it. That's all she had to do. He apparently became excited seeing a half-naked girl wearing his work shirt!

Then there are the Korean patrons, who tend to get excessively rowdy when drunk. "They are very rough, they swing girls from one end of the room to the other—they throw us! I really have no idea why. It's their culture or their nature. I don't know."

Jennifer's girls, the modern *geisha*, will pour your drinks, light your cigarettes, pamper you with hot towels, and sing along as Celine Dion warbles her *Titanic* theme tune. "My Heart Will Go On," ironically, underscores this scenario. KTV bars are still seen as dens of iniquity disguised as upscale watering holes. Some places will scam you S$50 for

90

a mug of beer. A private room can be procured for S$60, all night, but you'll have to pay lots of extras for the privilege. A bottle of Chivas Regal whiskey or Hennessy cognac costs S$300. A night out for two at one of the swankier Singapore KTV bars can easily cost S$2,000 at the end of the evening. Or S$8,000 if you bring a small entourage. You can hire a hostess for S$35 an hour, of which the *mamasan* will keep S$3; the girl gets S$26, the club the remaining S$6.

Selling beer or scotch at the bar keeps the action flowing, but the real game is to "target the bottles." At Jennifer's bar, the aim is to sell twenty-six bottles per night. In the first month it opened, they were doing only ten bottles a night and Jennifer blamed it on the ongoing economic downturn, which forced some of the other clubs in town to try and undercut the competition. One club in the Orchard Plaza area, she'd ruefully learned, was not only selling Chivas or Hennessy at half-price—S$150 a bottle—but it was also giving the room *free* with it, for the whole night!

"It's very competitive now, and very complicated too," she sighs. "People like us Malay girls because we are more 'happening.' Well, now you have these China girls and Indonesian girls spoiling the market. There are so many of them, and they will be 'happening' for just S$20! For my girls, if they strip and get naked, that's at least a S$50 tip. That's normal. My girls are not cheap, they are not *lorong* [back street] girls. My girls have been working for me for quite some time, and they really perform. If the girls want to have intercourse, it's up to them, but the minimum for 'short-time' should be S$250 and for just a blow job it should be S$150." It's the duty of the *mamasan* to set the minimum rates. "For me, I have higher expectations of these girls and I always advise the girls not to spoil the market," Jennifer insists. "I will ask at least S$200 for a girl, for 'short time.'"

In KTV parlance, 'short-time' means a quickie, usually a half-hour romp in the hay (or, in this case, on the leather). The *lorong* girls, the prostitutes who work in the legitimate brothels of Geylang, ply their trade in houses located on small side streets (*lorong* is Malay for "lane"); Geylang streets are named according to numerical order—Lorong 4, for instance, is famous for its Thai girls, Lorong 16 is where local men tend to go for their favorite mainland China girls.

"Yes, Geylang and all that, it's very straight-forward— you choose who you like and have sex—but here, it's a little more complicated," Jennifer sighs. "I build my base from regular customers who are comfortable with me. I also have two Russian girls, who are just a sideline for me, as social escorts. Some of these guests ask for Russian girls and I make the arrangements with this one pimp I know who has Russian girls. I get the girls from him and I get a commission from him. He has the girls but he doesn't have the clients. The clients are from here. These girls work on a 24-hourly basis—the guys take them at 3 p.m. and return them back at 3 p.m. the next day.

"For local girls, clients pay S$800 for twenty-four hours and I keep a commission of S$200. The girls make about S$400 and the rest goes to my club. For the Russian girls, the guys pay S$1,200 and I keep S$300. These two Russians are twenty-one and twenty-five years old. They come in as tourists and I bring them over to meet the clients. But they are on visitor's visas and I wouldn't want to get them or myself into trouble, so I only work with them twice a month. These girls don't work for agencies, they're on their own. And I keep that side of my business separate."

Jennifer pauses, lights another cigarette, and eyes the room with a wariness born of battle. The fact that she'd started out as a KTV hostess herself helps her to be a better *mamasan*, she says, because she understands the business. She isn't particularly keen on returning to the real world, back to the boring clerical job she held previously. But you deal with different parameters in a nightclub. "The business is not as good as before," she moans. "There are too many freelancers, all doing 'short-time,' blow jobs, all that. Some of them do 'short-time,' one shot, which used to go for S$500, and now you get them charging S$300. My girls do that too, but now it's a S$200 difference!

"Blow jobs are usually S$100 to S$150, and for 'short-time' it's S$300 to S$400. We don't take a cut from this. The guys come to the club and book the room, pay for the drinks, and then if he wants to do something sexual with the girl, the girl keeps everything. If they take the girl outside the club, that's called 'underbooking.' The minimum booking is two hours, at S$40 an hour. Fifty percent goes to the company and the rest goes to the girl, and she can negotiate anything else. They don't need to bring them back—the girl finds her own way back, but the cab fare to the hotel, or wherever, the customer has to pay that." At other clubs, a guy can extricate a girl from the premises during her evening work shift, but she has to be returned in two hours. The deal is always made with the *mamasan*, never the actual girl. Any girl who makes a private deal, to secretly date a customer, will be fired.

Jennifer frowns, discarding her earlier bravado. "It's difficult sometimes, especially for the new girls. I have to tell them, 'Okay, you have to talk. Conversation is very important. You have to keep on talking. If you can't talk to them, smile and sing with them, sing along. Unless they request for extra service, don't do it. Just pour drinks for them, dance with them, joke with them, entertain them. This is the entertainment business.' I have a lot of girls who are even married and I understand them, because I was once there. They get upset and go on about how men just want sex."

One girl, however, isn't complaining. A twenty-two-year-old nymphette named Rebecca suddenly emerges from one of the private rooms, runs up to Jennifer, and whispers something into her ear. "I have to go get a condom for Rebecca," Jennifer says as she excuses herself, looking a bit irked, perhaps because the gentleman didn't have the foresight to bring one. "We have condoms here, although we are actually not supposed to provide condoms," she adds. "The KTV license doesn't allow it."

Rebecca, Jennifer confides when she returns a few minutes later, "has the looks for the job—innocent but not so innocent. A lot of guys like that. The first time I saw her, I knew that. I said, 'I want her!'" Jennifer recruited the part-time telemarketer from her previous KTV bar, after they'd worked together for a few months. Rebecca, who says she's "100 percent pure Malay," still has not decided whether she will work full-time, but the four nights she puts in weekly generate enough quick cash to keep her at the club. Contrary to house rules, Rebecca occasionally makes the first move, which results in her feeling somewhat shameful if the guy rejects her. As if the very act of soliciting sex makes her feel like she's a whore.

"That's why I am still thinking about whether I should do this full-time," says Rebecca, some thirty minutes later, the deed well and truly done. "I have a lot of regulars now, some Japanese but most are local. Sometimes, they book me for 'outside' but I haven't gone, I'm a bit scared of that. I have never done a job 'outside' because I feel safe here. 'Outside' jobs are like escorting, which I would not do anyway, because of the timing. Sometimes I have to be here and sometimes I have to be there. Whereas when I work here, I can stay here one whole day.

"I get very normal guys, no toe-sucking or foot fetish or anything. Normally, they will tip S$50 to S$100 a guy. A blow job is around S$80 to S$100. Having sex is around S$150 to S$200. The whole thing takes two hours. We do karaoke first and then after that, after getting hot, then we will start." She bursts into a giggles.

"I know what she means," Jennifer interjects. "She gets close to them first, warms them up, rubs them there. So the guy will want more. And so, she makes the guy initiate it. The whole thing is to make the guy really want it. It works better that way. As time goes by, you learn and you get more professional."

Sometimes, Rebecca asks S$300 for sex, anticipating that the guy will try bargaining down. Even in an arena based upon primal instincts, strategies are to be deftly formulated, in an intricate dance of thrust and parry. "Who doesn't like sex?" Rebecca asks, rhetorically. "Sex is very important to me, I have desires. I like a little bit of pecking and necking, of course I do, but I don't like the guys who just get you in a room and just grope you right away. The last place I worked at, the guests were told that they were actually not obliged to give tips to the girls. Unless they really like you. Then, they're supposed to tip you discreetly. Very discreetly. Like they'll tuck the money inside my bra.

"And if a client booked me for a room, I would get a cut depending on the hours. The longer I got them to stay, the more money I got. On average, I would make an extra S$30 per hour, especially when they booked the room for the whole night and bought drinks. The biggest tip I ever got was S$400, for just having normal sex."

"Sometimes, I would perform 'all out'—perform for a group of guys in a room," she whispers. "My worst experience was with a guy who insisted on a blow job with no condom. He paid me S$100." The sound of her teeth gnashing couldn't be heard over Madonna singing "Ray of Light" over the club's PA but her sudden frown speaks volumes. "He was a regular at the club but he always tries new girls. He never asked for me again."

Yes, assistant *mamasan* Lena agrees, there are nights you just want to forget. She bums a cigarette off Jennifer, cagey about sharing some of the less salubrious aspects of her life story. Lena, twenty-five, hails from a working-class Malay family; she entered the business to help out her financially strapped sister. "I left school without finishing my O levels," she says. "My parents still don't know I am doing this. I tell them I work at a hair salon in the morning and, at night-time, in a factory. I used to work in the factory line with my mom, at Seagate, when I couldn't find any jobs after I'd left school. I lasted five months there. They wanted me to be a line leader, but I left. I couldn't see that as my career."

Lena is conscientious about her current line of work. "Making customers satisfied is important," she explains. "If they are satisfied they will want to come back again. I like to do doggie style, and to lick them all over." But every job has its limits. "I had a guy who was with a group of five other guys, and he wanted me to 'tiger-strip,' to do it with him in front of his friends. He was going to pay me S$5,000 plus an extra S$1,000 tip," Lena recalls. "But I was so scared. I couldn't do it! I told him, 'I'm sorry, sir, but I don't do this sort of thing.' I was so embarrassed."

The things one is compelled to endure for the sake of money. Most people don't think about the difference between an escort, a call girl or even a bar girl. But within the industry, the different labels are important. The career choices are quite varied, the ensuing emotional baggage always heavy, and one chooses according to what one can reasonably carry.

"After a while, you start to think about it," Jennifer admits. "But no. I won't do escorting. I have never seriously thought of escorting. It seems to me there are very high expectations involved in that job. It's very hard work. I'm not up to it. That, to me, is more like being a prostitute. I consider myself a 'high-class waitress.' A prostitute is someone who lingers around, looking for a customer. I guess, for me, it's not just about sex. It's about being able to entertain. I didn't understand any of that in my younger days. We are all really doing this because of the money, but there is a limit to what you will do for money.

"Some girls go to regular bars and pick up guys, they look for *ang moh* [white men]," she says, wearily. "Some girls get paid by guys who just want them to suck their toes." Where then do you draw the line, how do you extrapolate for definition and clarify fuzzy logic? "Back when I started, I didn't enjoy having to have sex with the guests that I didn't know at all. I still remember the first time. I followed the guy back to the hotel. Afterwards, I cried all the way home in the cab. Thinking of the fact that I needed money so much that I had to have sex for it. At first, it was hard to accept that."

"Yeah, I'm not cut out for escorting, either," Rebecca agrees. "The requirements are really high. You have to be a certain height, you can't be too fat, you can't be too skinny, you have to have a good complexion, blah, blah, blah. All that stuff."

Lena, however, is less chagrined: "I can see why people would say I am also a prostitute. But what people want to think, they can think. I'm just doing my job. If you want to disrespect me, go ahead. In this line, we study the guys, we know why they come here, we know what their problems are. They come here because they don't have company and they are bored at home. Some of them say their wives always nag them and they need somebody to talk to."

Despite having sex with customers for money on a nightly basis at the bar, sexually, Lena actually prefers women. She and Jennifer were once lesbian lovers and, though the relationship is no longer sexual, they still live together in a Marine Parade flat. And, at the club, they now work side by side but date other people. "With girls, it's so much better because we know our needs—which parts of our body needs it," Lena declares. "I have had girls offer to pay me but I usually never accept money for sex with them. I was asked to service another girl by a guy who offered to pay me for it. He offered me S$1,000 for the night. I didn't do it."

Like most sex workers, however, she'll usually divulge more if sufficiently pressed. The art of being secretive, after all, is what makes tantalizing the taste of forbidden fruit. "Okay, I've only done that once," she finally admits. "This woman paid me S$300 and we spent three hours together. She was someone who knew me from one of my previous jobs, before I got into the industry. I was a Hooters girl, at a

Hooters restaurant, and so was she. She confessed that she fancied me from that time, but I didn't notice it. I was working with her then and I just thought she was a good friend of mine. Nothing happened then, because I was going out with this guy at the time. But we went shopping together and stuff and it happened, she told me she loved me and all that. I had never done that before!"

Her breath sucks in just a tad, a tipple of sensual self-discovery, rendered exhibitionistic—what writer A.J. Benza once referred to as the "little whiff of denial all whores get high on." And for Jennifer and Lena and Rebecca, all Muslim-born Malay girls, making a living while doing the very things they're not supposed to—well, that surely begs some questions about denial; where these girls come from, drinking alcohol is forbidden, never mind sex for money.

"Yes, well, I would say I am not a strict Muslim, since I drink, and I would say I am probably very liberal," Rebecca says, a flash of silver darting from her mouth. "Yes, I'm also not supposed to have a stud in my tongue. But I do it because I want it, not because it's some kind of rebellion."

And what then does she think of the Malay escorts who are flown off for jobs in Brunei? She grunts. "No, I would never do that. I would not have sex with another Muslim for money."

Call that a conundrum, but it's emblematic of the contradictory mindset that applies to anything left-of-center in Singapore. Only in the country dubbed by William Gibson in *Wired* magazine as "Disneyland with the Death Penalty" would the sex industry be deemed legal yet not legitimized. "It's not legitimized because, no matter what, Singapore is still a conservative society," Rebecca says. "No matter what." The government has tried to stamp out illegal drugs by imposing hanging as punishment—the rock group R.E.M. once lampooned this when they came to Singapore in 1995, jamming at the Crazy Elephant blues club under the one-nighter name Mandatory Death Sentence—but those with contacts will assure you that anything can be bought. "It's so easy—you can get it free from the customers here," Jennifer discloses. "I was on heroin myself."

She isn't bragging; she nearly died because of it. "I was a very bad example," Jennifer says. "I even had sex when I was on it. And I was a *mamasan* the whole time! I think it was the pressure of the job that got to me. One time, the pressure was too much and I tried to kill myself. I slashed my wrists and I ended up in the ICU at the hospital, for four days. Lena came to see me. She was crying. I was lucky I didn't overdose. I've only been off heroin six months now. I don't need it. Some people get chills, some people get easily aroused. I didn't. Sex is the best drug there is. So I don't need it. Obviously."

"My life," she exclaims, feigning mock horror, "is so full of drama!"

Jennifer dissolves into another giggling fit. "I want to quit by the time I'm thirty. I'm twenty-eight now. Money is not everything. I lend a lot of the girls money, but they never pay me back. And my son, he doesn't know. He's nine now, going on ten. I'm not going to tell him. I don't ever want him to have this kind of idea, that his mother is this kind of person."

This kind of person? "Sometimes, you have to lose something to earn something," she says. The tiniest sliver of a tear trickles down. "I miss him a lot. My mother looks after him. She thinks I'm an office girl who goes to discos and goes clubbing. My dad doesn't know either. The thing is, I do this for the money and it's just a job. This is work. The part about getting paid for it, I have a little bit of a hard time with it."

She smiles briefly, that whiff of denial gently resurfacing. "Just a little bit."

Boys In The Hood

How I long for a lean man
Who is to say I do not deserve one?

—Cyril Wong, *Ann Siang Hill*

Like most writers, Cyril Wong, at age twenty-six, feels he has lived several lifetimes. For one thing, he's actually proud of the fact that he once worked as a gay social escort. It was a freelance, part-time avocation that began while he was an undergraduate at the National University of Singapore, where he completed his degree in English Literature with a dissertation on Singapore poet Arthur Yap. Today, he is an acclaimed poet himself, the winner of several awards who has brought fame to his home country, his work having been read in Australia (at the Queensland Poetry Festival), Hong Kong (at the Hong Kong International Literary Festival), the United States (at the Austin International Poetry Festival) and, most prestigiously,

Scotland (at the Edinburgh International Book Festival).

His work, Cyril says, "deals with self-humiliation and identity, the problematic nature of such emotions and the conventions of how we look at each other." His most recent books, *below: absence* and *Unmarked Treasure* are clearly entitled as ironic nods to the offbeat place of gay men in Singapore society.

Yet, unconventionally perhaps, he is no gay rights activist. None of the gay clubs that have sprung up all over town, with names like Backstage, Taboo, Club 95, and Water Bar, hold much fascination for him. He basically eschews the clichés of the gay lifestyle. "It is terrible but I feel bad not feeling really activist about it," Cyril sighs. "I guess I am just so tired because you spend your whole life dealing with it. I'm just doing it my own way, by promoting gay poetry. That's what I do and that's how I fulfill that side of me."

By day, Cyril works as a programmer at The Substation, the local arts center on Armenian Street that has become a noteworthy literary, performance, and visual arts collective, a coruscating prism for a small and somewhat disenfranchised minority, slogging away with underfunded, undervalued arts projects. He lives in a modest apartment in the Serangoon Road area, participates in local theater productions and sings with two vocal ensembles (the Singapore Youth Choir and the Baroque music group, Musica Obscura). Any spare time is spent assembling material for an anthology of gay poems, plays, and short stories—the planned sequel to the 2003 Singapore gay omnibus *People Like Us*—which he plans to edit at the end of 2004.

"I did escorting for four years, on and off," Cyril recalls over lunch at a restaurant in Raffles City. "Sometimes there would be nothing happening at all for two months, and then I would get calls from friends who knew guys who needed guys. A lot of the information will be exchanged on the Internet, so you know what he looks like or he knows what you look like, so you can just approach each other. I'd get paid upfront. We'd go to my place or go off for coffee or something."

But how exactly did it all begin? "There was a friend who was an escort, who was making S$500 an hour, and he said he could help me get contacts if I wanted to do my own thing," Cyril explains. "He was from Shanghai and he came here to study, I met him on the Internet. Aside from his regular escorting, he would meet up to have one-nighters on his own too, from meeting guys on the Internet. So that's how we met. We had a one-night stand and we got along really well. We got to learn a lot about each other. At the time, the reviews of my first book, *Squatting Quietly*, came out. And he went, 'You're not Chris, are you?' I went, "Um, yes." I don't use my real name—I'm 'Chris Tan'—on the Internet."

Thus began his pseudonymous escorting career, a ride that he would use to explore his own identity issues, particularly since most of his clients were foreigners. "My clients were usually businessmen stopping by Singapore, just looking for a good time, a lot of Japanese, one or two Swedes, three Americans, the rest mostly Malaysians," he remembers. "The *ang moh* I can count on the fingers of my hands, there weren't many." That's a surprising revelation, since a number of gay bars in Singapore are infamous hunting grounds for expatriate men desiring local boys. "No, I don't think it's the 'Asian boy' fantasy thing that they wanted from me. I always felt that I looked like an average teenager, and I remember feeling surprised that people would actually want to pay me for it. I think a lot of the clients were paying for sex because they couldn't get it elsewhere."

Therein lies one of the unwritten secrets of gay escorting: gay men are by nature extremely promiscuous, so the ones who pay for sex fall into one of two camps: they're either in high-level positions of corporate or political clout where, clearly, public outing would be disastrous or, more conventionally, they're too old to be out hustling for one-nighters on the gay club circuit. "And it's a bit sad that way," Cyril says. "Especially for the really older ones, the guys in their 50s. By older, I mean they're from thirty-six years old upwards. The oldest I had was fifty-seven. As a gay male escort, your clients will tend to be a lot older. A lot of times, the reason why they pay for it is because they're older and they don't have the appeal anymore or they know they're not going to get men by cruising and it's not like they can't afford to buy one. And they look it. You can sort of tell it's not really an exciting thing for them, doing it."

There's another difference between gay and straight escorting. "Gay people are different because we know what we're in it for—it's just sex," Cyril adds. "Gay men can draw that clean line between sex and emotion. For women, having sex for money can be a big deal but for us, it's not a problem. There is no angst about it. I even know of men who work as masseurs and are actually trained in massage. They get the clients to come to their houses and after the massage they will offer extra services for a fee. If you want an extra hand job, it's S$50 more. Anal will be S$100 more. That's another kind of 'escorting.' There's no 'money upfront' deal like the straight agencies do with their 'booking fees.' We just meet and discuss it as we go along, just bearing in mind that it's an hourly rate and money is time."

He laughs at this, shrugs a bit, the sensitive poet suddenly made self-aware, that he's maybe being too clinical about a taboo topic. He doesn't miss a beat when asked about his own rates. "For me personally, what I would charge by the hour depends. Sometimes it's S$300, inclusive of sex and anything else, including being tied up or whatever he wants. Just as long as he doesn't want to screw me with a garden tool or something like that, you know."

"I had a guy who wanted to be hit in the stomach," Cyril continues. "He wanted me to hit him, punch him in the stomach, and he would jerk off after that. I don't know why, and I don't get it. I've also done some SM jobs that involved tying them up and applying candle wax. But the funniest one was a guy who asked me to tape him up with Scotch tape. I would tape up his whole body and leave certain parts exposed so he gets more sensitive down there. And then, I can play with him sexually, and he would ask me to control his orgasm. Where he cannot come unless I say so. It took an hour or two, very tiring. And lot of Scotch tape! I had to buy a bunch at the 7-Eleven!"

And, like most escorts, it's all fun and games if you don't let love get in the way. It's a maxim about sex work that the sex worker has to draw his or her emotional boundaries or trouble will ensue. Cyril was careful with his dalliances until a particularly attractive client finally came along. "My most memorable one," is how he puts it now. "Somebody I kind of fancied. You tend to have one that you kind of fancy. The guy just didn't want it that way. He just wanted sex. I kind of liked him and wanted to go out with him a bit more. I almost declined being paid but I think he kind of suspected I liked him a bit more, so he ended the session a bit early." Cyril left the room devastated, an object lesson delivered in the ways and wherefores of compartmentalizing sex.

Cyril says he finally gave up escorting, because it was empty and futile. "I would leave the hotel room and go, 'What was that all about?'" he says. "I was also writing my first book at the time that I started escorting. It was very, very personal—writing the book was a way of sorting out a lot of personal issues for me—and there was a big emptiness in my life at the time and I didn't know how to fill it. The escorting thing came along at the right time to distract me." In the end, he recalls, "it was just very cold. I hated doing it myself. I don't know how women do it. I think there must be a difference between women and men when men do it or when my friends do it, but when I did it myself I just felt very horrible. I just feel really lonely at the end of the day. And the more I do such things, the more I realize I really do want a relationship. Right now, I am in a relationship. He knows about my past and he's okay about it."

Cyril's current partner of two years is public relations consultant Sheo S. Rai, thirty-three, a former civil servant who, in 2000, was asked to leave his government job because of his sexual orientation. At present, there are 60,000 employees in the Singapore civil service, the biggest employer in a country where the total number of people in the active workforce is 2.03 million, in a total population of 4.2 million. "I knew Cyril had been an escort," Rai says, over a beer at his favorite gay bar, Backstage, in Chinatown's Trengganu Street. "He tells me everything. What happened in the past is past."

He has never used escorts himself. "I was too afraid, and I didn't have money," he laughs. "I see escort agencies as providing a service. There's nothing wrong with that. I only have a problem if the boys or girls are forced into it against their will. Choice is very important thing. Gay escorts are fine for people who have problems picking up guys. Escort agencies are a perfect way for providing avenues for such people. You have to pay to have someone to spend time with, but I think it's good. Whatever you suppress, it will come out some way or other so I would rather have this kind of thing be out in the open."

What usually makes gay sex controversial is its recreational nature: it is activity that has no reproductive function, and this usually draws the ire of conservatives. "Gay men are having sex all the time," Cyril notes. "Sometimes we'd do what a lot of gay men would call 'charity cases'—where we have sex with men we don't really like but they kind of like us so we'd go, 'Okay, I'll do this for you even though I'm going to get only 10 percent of the pleasure that you're feeling. You get through them by thinking about other things. The whole physical thing, I think, is a male thing. Like we can block out the emotional side of it, at least for a while. It works fine for us, especially since there is so little repeat business in gay escorting. There are so many gay men out there. They all just come and go.

"Sexually, I don't usually have any performance issues. I get horny really easily. It's up the client what he wants to do if he has performance problems. We can cuddle, we can talk. If nothing happens, nothing happens, I will just be around. I heard a story from a friend about how this old guy couldn't get it up the entire night. He couldn't get it up—it was like for two hours! My friend said he just kept trying but it was very, very tiring. More tiring than having sex!"

Facilitating that frenetic nexus of commerce is the gay pimp, guys like Eddie Mui, twenty-nine, a Hong Kong native. On most days, he's seen hopping in and out of MRT stations, checking out some of his new boys working cruising grounds like Wheelock Place, in and around the pedestrian mall area where Scotts Road, Orchard Road, and Orchard Boulevard meet. Eddie grew up in suburban Clearwater Bay, out in the New Territories in Hong Kong, not a poor boy by any means. But he was forced to channel his teenage rebellion into visible means of support when his father kicked him out of the house for smoking pot. The gay pimping scene didn't cut it for him in Hong Kong, so he bought a one-way ticket to Singapore, where he now has a regular day job ("in the fashion industry," though he won't say exactly where) and moonlights as a pimp almost as a hobby.

"I started out just trying to help my friends because I thought the other pimps were making too much money from it," he says. "I'm not like one of those pimps where you take half—I mean, some pimps will take S$1,500 if the client pays

S$3,000 and, to me, that's too much. You didn't do anything, you know, so what are you taking S$1,500 for? For me, the split is usually seventy-thirty, with the 30 percent going to me. The other pimps, some of them will go up to you on the MRT train and give you a card and go, 'You're really good looking.' Then they will ask if you want to make more money and tell you they'll offer you a sixty-forty split, where you take 40 percent."

The work offers the usual variations on a theme, which Eddie loves to disclose with a fast-gun, earnest fervor. "One guy paid $3,000 for two hours, and my cut was S$500. The guy was very nice, even though he was a very old guy, and he took the boy out to dinner and all that. But I did get a job for an escort of mine that involved asphyxiation. When he was doing the guy, or when the guy is jerking off, he wants to be choked."

Eddie has been in the game three years, and he made all his initial contacts like Cyril did, on the Internet. "I was very amateurish in the beginning, when I got to Singapore. I was, like most gay boys, very active on the Internet. And then a friend of mine said, 'Hey, it's so easy to be a pimp now, so why don't you do it?' I had a lot of friends whom I knew some older guys would really like so I helped them to get contacts on the Internet, on sites like *SG Boy*, *Gay Teens*, and so forth. I had clients offering S$1,000 to S$3,000 an hour. Sometimes S$3,000 just to keep them company, just like regular escorting."

Eddie scoffs at the big escort agencies that advertise in the *Yellow Pages* claiming to offer both men and women. For gay men who need a pimp, that route is financially disastrous. "Those escort agencies are the ones where they take a really big cut and you only join these agencies if you're not really in the know and you're desperate for money," Eddie says. "Once you join those agencies and you come out, you really know you've been ripped off, since you can actually do it on your own."

The straight escort scene, he admits, "is more glamorous, since they have this whole deal with the booking fee and extra money for extra activities." Gay escorting, Eddie explains, is best done through an informal, underground network of reliable contacts. "And then I would say, 'Okay, he's going to meet you at Wheelock Place, the downstairs area.' That area has a lot of cruising, I don't know why, since they don't really hang out anywhere." Eddie started out with just two guys and then he had six, making anywhere from S$50 to S$500 per job, going by his seventy-thirty split rule.

"Getting S$500 is actually quite rare," he admits. "The

practice is usually that the pimp gets more but I never made that a practice for myself. It was a personal thing. I never took more than 30 percent. It's not like straight escorting where you feel you deserve that much money because the escort has never done it before and they need you. Where gay escorts are concerned, I think they all have."

Eddie agrees with Cyril about the recreational nature of gay sex as the major arbiter of demand and supply: "A lot of the issues that come up in straight escorting just don't come up with us. It's very different for gay men. It's so easy, emotionally, and it's so easy to get clients."

"If anyone wanted advice from me about doing escorting," Eddie now says, "I would say come to me if you want phone numbers to call. And then, rule number one, don't give your real name. And then, don't give your cellphone number. Don't work without using protection. Don't give out your number by calling them—you contact me. If the client gets there and can't find you, he will call me and then I will call you to say, 'Hey, where are you? He's there already!'"

Indeed, the customers are already there, all over the place, which is why some people in the gay community don't understand what the big deal is. True, as a gay person, your whole life often becomes unnecessarily politicized, but does the politics of gay escorting necessarily confer an extra sense of frisson? "This is a phenomenon everywhere," says Jeff W., thirty, a Singaporean gay lawyer, who requests anonymity because of his work (he represents some heavy-duty financial institutions). "If you ask an escort agency, they will tell you, 'I only hire them out as social escorts, as companions. What they decide in their private time is their business.' It's a very common answer. It's only a gray area simply because we all know what's going on there, but we can't prove anything. But in this regard, there should be no difference between gay escorts and straight escorts. Frankly, what's to stop someone from having a registered house of male prostitutes? If you don't post a policeman outside every which way, what's to stop anyone from coming in? Men could come in and just sit in the living room—they wouldn't know. There's nothing illegal about that."

"I think we should legalize escorting in general," Jeff says, "because there's no way you're going to stop it anyway. People are going to have sex, and people are going to pay for sex because they need it. Frankly, I would rather make sure that we minimize the dangers and the negative effects of sex crimes by making it all above-board and registered. In the event of a sex crime, the escort involved can come forward."

Much ado was made in the Singapore press about gays in the civil service after Prime Minister Goh Chok Tong's unprecedented, compassionate statement in July 2003, as reported in the Singapore tabloid *The New Paper*, appealing for the gradual acceptance of gay people. Singaporeans, the report cited Goh as saying, would "understand that some people are born that way...We are born this way and they are born that way, but they are like you and me." He might have been referring to the genetic evidence surrounding the Xq28 chromosome, which scientists say determines male sexuality, but he was also divulging an open secret—that there have been gays in the civil service all along, anyway.

"Well, we're not special in any other way other than the sex part, right?" Jeff W. retorts. "Of course, from the government point of view, it makes sense. This whole thing is geared towards seeing what the public reaction will be like. And possibly, to slowly consier decriminalization. But I'm a political realist. The government has never, ever done anything they've wanted to do in one giant leap. It's always been very, very small baby steps, all the way. It's a slow, unfolding process. But it's going to miss my generation." He's already planning to emigrate to his favorite city, Vancouver, Canada, which already has a built-in ambience of

119

social acceptance for the gay male.

At the heart of the debate is the whole issue of why the government would openly endorse gay citizens without decriminalizing gay sex. According to Sections 377 and 377A of the Singapore Penal Code, any act of homosexuality is an offense. And, on the legal forefront, Article 12 of the Singapore Constitution omits mention of either gender or sex: "There shall be no discrimination against citizens of Singapore on the ground only of religion, race, descent or place of birth in any law or in the appointment to any office or employment..."

"Yes, you can be gay but you cannot engage in the act," comments Cyril's partner Sheo, the ex-civil servant. "I think the Prime Minister knows that but his hands are tied. I don't blame him. After thirty-seven years of independence, finally a leader acknowledges our existence. We exist! And that is a momentous occasion for me. I cannot ask for more right now. It's unrealistic to ask for more. A lot of gay groups take on a very competitive stance, which is unproductive. If you want to have things change, you have to work their way, work towards incremental changes. You can't have revolutionary, sudden change."

"I was closeted myself, and didn't hang around gay

people," he recalls. "I knew I was gay when I was twelve or thirteen. I forced myself to like girls but somehow guys appealed to me. I've never had a relationship with a woman. I relate to girls more emotionally and intellectually rather than physically. My first relationship was three years ago, when I was twenty-nine. When I joined the civil service department at twenty-five, I hadn't been in a relationship yet. I just knew I was gay. My family still doesn't know."

Cyril says they both like the thrill of the forbidden, even though in the Singapore context it comes with some extra twists and turns. "Yes, definitely, when it's taboo, it's more interesting, but I realize now that being Singaporean is a real concept," he says. "Something called 'Singaporean'—this unthinking, T.S. Eliot 'Hollow Man' thing, really. People become that too, they form their own versions of it. It's very creepy. I'll go to gay clubs like Taboo and get really disgusted sometimes. Gay people are marginalized, and they have formed their own subculture too, to the point where they'll say, 'This is what being gay is about. If you're not like that, what's wrong with you?' It's elitist in a very physical sense—it's all about looks, it's all very visual. Within this monolithic thing, they actually believe Malays don't have prospects like the Chinese do, and Indians even much less, even in the gay community. They don't like each other very much."

Given the Singapore political context, the gay escort or the gay pimp stays quietly in the shadows. The mainstream sees them as figures of questionable integrity, in a subculture of questionable worth. Dr. Stuart Koe, another former civil servant and now the Founder/CEO of the Asian gay website *Fridae* (*www.fridae.com*), believes that "the gay escort scene exists here but it's very underground. They're not very above-the-line like they are in Sydney or in New York or in London, where the city papers have a very thick back section with ads for call boys and call girls. That doesn't happen in Singapore. But a lot of the escort agencies cater to tourists, because the escorts go to the hotels. I also know there are certain 'agents'—they prefer to be called that rather than 'pimps'—who will bring boys in and they do have a client list where they'll call up to say, 'Look, I've got someone new in, would you like to meet them?'"

But don't call Cyril Wong for advice. He's out of that game for good. Most of his escorting experiences didn't translate successfully as poetry. "The people I met through escorting were very interesting and I wrote a lot of poems about that, but I was never very satisfied with any of it," he says. "The poems were all catalytic, they were cathartic, but they didn't really solve anything. It just didn't work. I don't know why. Even up to this day, I still wonder why." But he still likes some of them, like "Flight Dreams," which made it into his recent fourth book, *Unmarked Treasure*:

> *I often dreamt of flying when I was younger.*
> *Such dreams supposedly meant*
> *that I had feelings of entrapment in my real life.*
> *It was true. Back then, I believed*
> *I was determined to lead a life*
> *my parents would be proud of: I would attain*
> *a degree, a job, remain a Christian, marry a nice girl.*
> *During those days, I would fly*
> *off balconies, jump off the tops of flats and swim*
> *through air for hours in my sleep.*
> *Then I discovered a part of me that rose up*
> *in a hundred bedrooms that eventually*
> *looked like each other, when a stranger's*
> *hand or mouth would push me back into myself,*
> *only to suck me back out again by the shock*
> *of the body's capacity for desire*

That capacity for desire, with all the pain that comes with pleasure, is what he sought to understand. "I don't do any of this anymore," Cyril now says of escorting, with the world-weariness of the retired sex worker. "Even now, I still get phone calls. But I don't do anything about them. And I don't answer phone calls where I don't recognize the numbers."

Victoria's Secrets

Professional domination is physically clean in
that the client doesn't get to leave his fingerprints
all over your body. But he leaves his fingerprints
all over your soul.

—Ernest Greene

Ten years ago, Victoria was an escort in her native Hong Kong, working the smoky bars of Wanchai and Tsim Sha Tsui. Following a string of relationships, one rocky marriage, and an illicit affair, she was introduced to the world of BDSM (bondage-discipline/sado-masochism) and felt something stir deep inside. Victoria became Empress Victoria, professional dominatrix, who flies down occasionally to Singapore to conduct sessions out of five-star hotels. Her most active market is the United Kingdom, but, unlike some Hong Kongers, she won't sneer at Singapore; not when there are clients who will grovel at her feet, kiss the ground she walks on, and, most importantly, pay her upscale rates. She charges each overseas client HK$15,000 (about S$4,000) per day, excluding plane ticket and hotel accommodation; this is usually paid upfront, plus a 30 percent security deposit. In Hong Kong, she charges HK$2,500 per hour, each session lasting anywhere from two to six hours.

"Some of my clients like to be discreet," says Victoria, "so they choose for me to work out of their hotel room rather than in a dungeon. It depends on the scene and the client's fantasies. If he wants a 'female boss' or 'French maid' fantasy, a hotel room is more appropriate than a dungeon. If I am working on a masochist or doing interrogation, I prefer a dungeon." Previously, most of her clients came from an advertisement she placed in *www.alt.com*, but now she gets them from her own website, *www.empressvictoria.org*, which extols the "Mysteries of Oriental Domination" with the command: "Praise my beauty and worship my whip." She specializes in "psychodrama, interrogation, discipline, mental torture, mind control, verbal humiliation, corporal punishment, whips, canes, CBT, paddles, cat-o'-nine-tails, needles, piercing, hot wax, and anal torture."

Yes, you can also call her Mistress Victoria, if the "Empress" honorific conjures up images of frumpy dowagers. Frumpy she is not, at age thirty-four. Her home-page on her site warns that she is not to be trifled with. "If you are looking for someone to have sex with or if you are a BDSM tourist, boy, DO NOT WASTE YOUR TIME," read the opening lines. (When clicked, the exit link sends you straight to the *Official Harry Potter Homepage*!) There are letters of endorsement from her slaves, like Erick from Amsterdam and Thomas from London (who writes "with a burning desire to be again at your entire disposal, dear Empress").

One of her favorite clients is a prominent society lawyer who treats her to massive shopping sprees; she once spent HK$40,000 of his money at Louis Vuitton in Hong Kong, in a single afternoon. Victoria knew she had him under her control when he passed his first test.

"We had coffee at the Ritz-Carlton," she remembers. "I asked him to move his ass to the coffee shop to meet me, and he was surprised because I was rude but I knew he liked it. I wasn't in a commercial mood that day so we just had dinner and chatted. For the rest of the week, he kept sending me about fifty SMS messages a day. Whenever I had free time in Central, even half-an-hour, he would run down from his office just to see me! I didn't feel the pressure until one

Sunday when I was sick at home and he kept sending me stupid SMS messages again, like: 'I miss you, where are you?' and 'Why don't you talk to me? Did I do something wrong? I want to kiss you. I want you.'

"It was just bizarre. For Christ's sake, I was sick and having a temperature! I told him I wasn't feeling well. He just panicked and thought I was leaving him. So I changed my tone and sent him a text message: 'My dear boy, Mistress thinks you deserve the worst punishment on the planet: Abandonment. Unless you follow my instructions.' And I called up the sales girl at Chanel and asked her to reserve a handbag which cost HK$11,800 and a cashmere shawl which cost HK$5,800, and then I sent him another message. I asked him to go to the shop and pay for the stuff. And he did, with respect. What an obedient boy!"

She also has a client in China, a European living in the Sichuan town of Yichang, an industrial area nestled amid the Chang Jiang forests and the bucolic Yangtze Three Gorges. With him, the area of expertise deployed is usually CBT (cock/ball torture). "He is a very good, handsome man, not very tall but very well-dressed, with beautiful blue eyes," Victoria reveals. "We don't do any role-play, no music, just a quiet session, highly concentrated, highly erotic. He likes piercings around his scrotum and penis. I like working with him because it turns me on so much. He also likes heavy CBT—I nail his balls to a piece of wood, whip him on his pierced spot till it bleeds. I need special equipment to do that, because of hygiene. He has his own private whip and lot of medical equipment. An absolute masochist!"

During their very first session, they had an accident, an unexpected baptism-by-fire that, paradoxically, only enhanced their mutual enthusiasm. "After I'd finished the fifth piercing on his scrotum, we both got really excited," recalls Victoria. "He begged me to put a piercing on his foreskin. I said no because he was aroused and also, there are too many blood vessels around that area and he might bleed badly. But he started kissing me, saying the nicest things in his native language, and I was aroused by the tone of his voice. So I surrendered.

"I put my latex gloves on, lay him down, cleaned him up with iodine and alcohol. My heart was pounding. I was still soaking wet but also trying to concentrate, a complicated emotional alteration! Both of us got really excited and everything went well at the beginning. I always use rings instead of barbells for piercings, so half of the needle went through his foreskin and then I attached the ring, following through nicely. But when the ring was going through the flesh, halfway through, he started to bleed. I wanted to get it done and clean up, so I pushed the ring against the needle a bit quicker than usual, which is also a quick way to avoid too much pain. Unfortunately, the ring and needle detached in the middle of the flesh—the needle went through, but half of the ring was stuck in the foreskin. I was annoyed and nervous but kept my face calm, waiting for my client to panic or scream or jump around. I also mentally prepared for the CPR, to call the ambulance and then go to jail.

"We just looked at each other, speechless. Surprisingly, he didn't make a single noise. He even had a smirk on his face and winked at me, while I was panicking and thinking about what I should do next!

"I decided to take the ring out, because the last thing I wanted was to be going to the hospital and becoming the local newspaper headline the next day. So I took a deep breath and took the ring out. As expected, his penis was bleeding like a fountain. Before I could try to put anything on him to soak the blood and stop the bleeding, he said, 'It's okay, it's okay, don't worry,' and ran off to the bathtub and started rinsing himself.

"It took God-knows-how-long to stop the bleeding. He

walked out from the bathroom, holding his penis, came to me and showed me the wound. 'Look, it's okay now, don't worry,' patting my shoulder with his warm hand while I collapsed on the chair. The room looked like a murder scene. I felt pretty sure he must've been born in another dimension or on another spiritual ramp or something. He's definitely not Martian."

There is a gleam in her eyes when she talks about such things, something beyond words, very feral and primal. The kind of look that tells you, unequivocally, that she's the real thing. Not at all like the Singaporean escorts who, if called upon, will do the odd domination job here and there, mostly asphyxiation, maybe also some naff spanking and twee paddling ("Just a bunch of girls with whips," as one European expatriate based in Singapore, a BDSM practitioner, complained). No, she marches to the beat of a very different drum, though some of her work has parallels to escorting.

"A six-hour session doesn't mean I will beat the client up for six hours," she clarifies. "It will include some other activities. I take him to places like restaurants and bars with his chastity belt on. Sometimes I will organize something with the restaurant especially for the client."

"This is not an easy job, really," Victoria smiles, "since I have to be creative." But she knows her market value; amid the professional ranks of BDSM culture, the sheer presence of a born-and-bred Hong Kong Chinese dominatrix is distinct and unusual, let alone the fact that she can be contacted through her website, with plenty of photos of herself for public viewing. And then, there are the letters she receives, litanies of requests ranging from the amusingly strange to the downright bizarre, but all very sincere and touching.

For instance, a new client saw her advertisement on a UK Mistresses website and wrote to ask for an appointment in London. "My main interests are trample and boot/shoe worship," he emailed. "May I ask if you offer boot/shoe worship? As much as I enjoy licking/kissing costume boots and shoes I would much rather you make me clean a pair of your everyday footwear. Would this be possible? I will lick clean anything you like: boots, shoes or trainers. I recently licked a woman's boots clean that were caked in dried mud. I felt a bit rough for a couple of days afterwards, but am keen to do it again.

"As for trample, I have had quite a few sessions in the past and enjoy all aspects—high heel, stocking, bare foot, head-standing, face-smothering, etc. I hope to be able to take what you offer. One thing I would love to try is having one of your well-worn shoes or trainers strapped over my nose and mouth whilst you trample me. Have you ever done this? Would you do it? Other fantasies are drinking out of your worn footwear and being forced to suck on your well-worn insoles, from your boots or trainers. I would also be interested in having you spit into my mouth during the session. May I ask if this is something you are happy to do?"

Happy? Victoria's beside herself. "I borrowed a friend's three-year-old trainer, a shoe which was extremely smelly— ugh, I don't even want to talk about it," she sighs. "I get a lot of boot/shoe fantasies like that one. Some of them can suck and lick my feet for hours. I had a client who liked to peek while I was washing and massaging my feet. He would wank himself off outside the bathroom."

Even while sipping iced tea in an alfresco café in Singapore, her luminous black hair blowing in the breeze, Victoria has an elfin charm about her that belies anyone's notion of a self-contained, self-possessed woman who doles out corporal punishment. Like her peers, she can wax lyrical about "therapeutic spanking techniques" and "age-play regression spanking" for those "held in bondage by their

•

sacred spanking fantasies."

"I started out working at Club Versailles in Wanchai, from 1985 to 1989, where I trained as a hostess," she begins. "I learned how to drink spirits and not get drunk, how to dress up and be presentable and, of course, how to be good in bed. That was the Golden Age of the sex industry in Hong Kong, when everybody made a lot of money through the stock market and real estate, so we didn't have to provide sexual services to get good tips. At that time, when my clients wanted to get intimate, he had to pay a lot of money. I was very young, eighteen years old, and that was only my first stage in the sex industry."

A fifty-three-year-old shipping magnate took a shine to her and extricated her from the nightclub. "He took care of me and I did some studying and had a normal job as a secretary for a couple of years," she recalls. "But we didn't work out in the end and, in 1992, I decided to go back to Club Versailles. In early 1993, I left to work at Club Bboss in Tsim Sha Tsui East. Club Versailles's business was going downhill and we hardly made any money. I needed a break from Hong Kong and left the club at the end of 1993, and relocated to Sydney, Australia, where I furthered my studies and finished an advertising degree. I also worked as an escort in a gentlemen's club on Pitt Street.

"The club's still there but under a different owner now— the previous owner killed himself right there in the club with a handgun, in 1995," she adds, trembling slightly at the memory. "I got really depressed in 1995. And escorting in Sydney is so different from Hong Kong. We worked in shifts. Crazy hours, 6 p.m. to 2 a.m., and we also had to pay a fine if we were ever late. The club was beautiful, though, well-decorated, and some girls looked like fashion models."

Respite from the depression came in the form of yet another man, a wealthy American client from Pennsylvania who took her back to the United States, where they lived together for a year. However, things didn't quite pan out yet again and she found herself back in Hong Kong in 1997, a few months before the crown colony fell back to Chinese rule. Victoria worked as an escort in the evenings but quit to open her own jewelry shop; she designs her own jewelry and is also an aromatherapist.

And then, she met a European man working in Hong Kong, who became her husband. "We got married in December 2001 and life was normal," she says, with an ironic laugh. "He is not in the scene. He is open-minded about it, but not interested. My husband is a caring, open minded, intelligent man and I adore him so much. He's absolutely a gift from God." When she's off on one of her overseas jaunts, he usually flies to mainland China for some rounds of golf. "He doesn't know about my past life," she notes, referring to her escorting career.

Things took a fateful turn in mid-2002, when the marriage hit a bump in the road and skidded. Victoria plunged into an affair, not just with a new man but with the BDSM world. "He was the one who opened the door," she now says. "The third time we had sex, he started to spank me and he put a collar on me, I was so excited! I liked it when he put me on a leash and treated me like a cat. I walked like a cat. I found I liked to be whipped and spanked and being called a slut.

"It was heaven! I was sure then, that I was born to play BDSM!"

Victoria discovered the famous Hong Kong BDSM haven Fetish Fashion, which operates somewhat incongruously out of a space it cheekily calls "the Cockloft," on busy Cochrane Street in Central. It's a clean, well-lit place, where one can procure an array of latex and leather apparel, amid displays of colored condoms and lace teddies. The BDSM play parties are held downstairs, in the basement dungeon, where all the deeper, darker accoutrements of the trade are on view: a St. Andrew's cross where one can be tied and whipped; body bags on the walls, to encase those fond of sensory deprivation; even a cage, snug enough for a fully-grown man on all fours.

Victoria came. She saw. She was home.

"I started as a submissive," she explains. "I am naturally submissive in daily life, and I found that I wanted to change. So I found Fetish Fashion and went to one of their play parties, on my own. I didn't know what to expect but, at that time, being a sub felt safer, because I didn't have a clue what was going on and didn't know what to expect. And, during the party, I saw a beautiful Asian dom with a whip in her hand. She looked stunning! She looked into her slave's eyes and spoke to him softly: 'Get me a drink.' She was natural, she didn't yell or shout to show her power. Very sophisticated.

"I was fascinated. I said to myself, 'That's what I want! I want to be like her!'"

She asked Fetish Fashion's intrepid owner, Mistress Decima, to train her. Decima, of course, had gained more than fifteen minutes of infamy when she was arrested in October 2001. Five undercover policemen had been planted at one of her play parties and twenty-three policemen had raided the place, complete with crow bars and video cameras, confiscating clothing and hauling everyone off to the station—for supposedly "giving a live, objectionable public performance." They were released on bail after twelve hours, and then formally charged. The ensuing trial took slightly more than a year to complete, whereby Fetish Fashion was accused, as Decima herself puts it, "under an arcane British law" of "keeping a disorderly house."

But no sexual intercourse had actually taken place, and the judge admitted he was bewildered. He couldn't grasp the fact that BDSM doesn't include any actual genital contact. Where was the fun in that? All the charges were thrown out and the accused acquitted.

And so, luckily for Victoria, Decima and Fetish Fashion stayed in business. "Decima interviewed me in Lan Kwai Fong, in March 2003," Victoria recalls. "I told her I wanted to do something different, that could give me a good income, and I was willing to learn. That's how I started, with the original intention of also using it to dominate my husband. My first training was funny. Decima and I couldn't find a proper slave that day so Mistress Loretta, the shop's manager, got us a foot slave instead.

"I was dying to learn how to whip and spank and flog,

but the slave was only interested in toe-sucking and foot-licking. I was stuck because we have to respect the slave's limits. Finally, he agreed to let me practice flogging and spanking on him, so I learned something from Decima in the end. After that, I started browsing websites and buying books from Amazon, learning how to be a dom. I also visited one of the British doms and learned how to mentally control a slave and other punishment skills. Because of my previous experiences, I was very open to new things and it wasn't too hard to pick up the skills."

Imagery of BDSM has been superficially co-opted into mainstream pop culture—think Dolce & Gabbana, think Madonna, Britney Spears, Christina Aguilera, and even the folk-pop siren Jewel, all dolled up in corsets, garters, and gloves (Jewel even wore one for the cover of *Blender* where her glove sheathed only one finger, her middle, "birdy" digit). Even in Singapore, when the local media got in on the game, the usually conservative *The Straits Times* ran a teasing color photo of thespian Beatrice Chia after she'd won the DBS Life! Theatre Awards "Best Director" prize (for her controversial play *Shopping and F***king*); she appeared dressed in black, legs encased in fishnet stockings, whip in one hand. And the provocative headline,

"Who Says I'm a Man-eater?"

In reality, however, the general public has at best a scant understanding of what a professional dominatrix actually does.

True doms and subs are people who utilize BDSM to cauterize their psyches. They re-enact fantasies as a way of receiving therapy, either by dominating someone or submitting to someone. In the words of bondage video director/producer and *Taboo* magazine editor, Ernest Greene: "They quickly learn that it's not just smacking some butts and collecting some money. Your ability to navigate someone's fantasy and to bring some freshness and creativity to it over time is what builds a regular relationship. And regular clients are the key to the business, just like any other business.

"What a dominant really does is quite different from what you see in movies. It's not just a woman getting dressed up, cracking her whip, and saying, 'Grovel at my feet, you worm.' Most clients have far more specific and detailed needs than that...Looks are nice but they're not as important as a dominant's ability to connect to the desires of men who are often filled with shame and confusion about what they want."

And that's where things get metaphysical. As Fetish Diva Midori, the BDSM icon, parses the terminology, "Dominatrix is a profession or a performance, dominant is a state of being." Midori, the star of several BDSM movies including *Cruel Beauty* and *Dark Paradise*, also teaches classes across the United States entitled "The Art of Feminine Dominance." To her, it is all about the celebration of beauty, which she defines as "confidence, grace, posture, and presentation." Paul Theroux spent 5,000 words in an article published in *The New Yorker* deconstructing the dynamics of such curious wonderment; his piece dramatically began with an account of a man whose favorite fetish was to have a female dominatrix crush and kill insects with her stiletto-heeled shoe while he masturbated.

It's a mindset that the veteran practitioners all understand. Mistress Decima of Fetish Fashion will hold court, if you're ever interested, about her personal instrument of choice, the "single-tail"—akin to a bullwhip, the cause of much bodily harm if not used with consummate skill. The legendary Mam'selle Victoire of New York, now retired, will rhapsodize about her specialty, the cane, and how it must land with millimeter precision and sufficient force to just ever so slightly break the skin.

Accordingly, when Mistress Victoria of Hong Kong tells of her specialties and preferences, her words are precise and loaded. "I am very good at role-play and psycho-drama, and my sessions are sensuous and dramatic," she claims. "However I don't believe a dom should be yelling and bitching around to show her power. In terms of fetishes, I like rubber, PVC, and leather. And I like to integrate more severe punishment into my sessions these days, such as needle play and piercing. I do it for medical scenes or I just fake it to scare the hell out of the more rebellious, arrogant clients. I make sure no one can escape from my interrogation!"

"Professional domination has a built-in benefit that's absent in every other type of sex work," observes Lily Burana, author of *Strip City*, in a brilliant piece on BDSM culture for *Penthouse* magazine ("An Embarrassment of Bitches," January 1999). "Its tough-girl veneer affords the work force something of a social buffer against the judgement-prone—if not respect, at least a respectful distance. Because the image of the dominatrix is a woman in complete control, and there is generally a minimum of nudity and intimate physical contact involved, professional domination does not carry the same takes-all-comers 'fallen woman' stigma as prostitution, stripping, or porn modeling. Plus, there's an intimidation factor: People are less likely to fuck with you if they think you could—and happily would—kick their ass."

Victoria likes to quote from Anthony Minghella's film *The Talented Mr. Ripley*: "Everybody should have one talent. What's yours?" She's discovered hers and intends to continue exploring its riches, though with a wistful sigh she admits that she wishes more people would understand what women like her do, and what they bring to the male-female dance. Sure, money is transacted, but it isn't her real end-goal. "It is the energy-interaction between me and the client during the session. When my client and I click, every word I say becomes magic. Every single touch gives him the chills. Pain becomes ecstasy. And that's what I call fulfilling. There's nothing quite like a client's appreciation. A long hug after the session can be something memorable."

"I am a very sensual and sexual person," she says, "and I never hide this part of me from anybody. I am proud of being who I am and what I do. Social norms, what's that? I see them as an excuse for people to be judgmental."

Her tolerant husband, she admits, hides a jealous streak and she takes great pains not to discuss her sessions. "What he doesn't like is the intimate conversations between me and the clients—our talking about their fantasies and stuff," she lets on, after a pregnant pause. "My passion for being a good dom actually creates a gap between us. We are trying hard to work that out at the moment." At the time of writing, however, Victoria was in the midst of relocating to London and divorcing him. "He can play the dom when he gives me money," she mutters dryly. "After my training, I used some of my techniques on him and it seemed to work pretty well, but it didn't really change his path, which is very vanilla."

"I am a pro dom who wears Armani," asserts Victoria. "I have learned and grown from BDSM. I have no problem admitting that I am an extravagant woman and I like to be glamorous." But she cites her hobbies as "golf, traveling and reading. I travel a lot, both for pleasure and business. My most fascinating trip was Egypt, I went there in 2000, and I plan to visit Tibet next. And as far as reading is concerned, I read all sorts of books about BDSM but my favorite books are *The Power of Now* by Eckhart Tolle and *Conversations with God* by Neale Donald Walsch. Books about personal enlightenment and spirituality."

Domination, Victoria says, has sharpened her senses to the palliative power of sex work, heightening her awareness of her abilities and where they intersect with the needs of her clients. "You definitely need self-awareness when you're doing this kind of work," she says. "If you're working without passion, and if you're full of shame and guilt about yourself, you can become abusive and over-powering. And what sort of dom you think that would be?"

Not a good one, in her book. This is serious business. "I don't recall anybody getting beaten up who'd dare to laugh about it." She starts to take her leave, saying she has to get back to the hotel, to await the visit of a new slave, for another session. There is a small community of kindred spirits in Singapore, but she's here to work, with no intention of attending any of their play parties.

"I actually have no connection with the BDSM scene *per se* in Singapore," she says. "I am most active in the United Kingdom—I've found the English to be the most sophisticated players, with the right attitude about the whole thing. My clients in Singapore are the ones who have seen my profile on the Internet and they'll invite me to come here and give sessions, usually in my hotel room. It's simple really, as long as they pay for the air fare and accommodation." Straight sex with a client, which she prefers to call a "power exchange," is a rarity, usually spontaneous and unplanned.

"Sometimes when I get hungry, I just eat anything on the menu," she laughs. "Not a good habit at all."

And with that, she's off to the taxi stand, to catch a quick pre-session warm-up exercise. A different kind of power exchange: "Louis Vuitton, at Takashimaya Orchard," she discloses, thanks to a very generous client from last night. An Australian based here in Singapore, who paid for two hours of bondage. She tied him to the bedposts, stuffed his briefs into his mouth and gave him what he most desired: verbal humiliation.

"The only pleasure left in your otherwise worthless life," she reminded him.

Later, with the session over, he offered to personally take her to Ngee Ann City, to Louis Vuitton. But Victoria rebuffed him with a sultry sneer that evidently, quickly, turned him on.

She simply stared at his renewed erection with all the contempt that a mistress should reward a quivering slave.

"I'm always on my own," she told him. "And I like to keep it that way."

PART THREE

Risqué Business

Girls, Food, Lodging

It's hard to decipher the difference between
a sincere entertainer and an honest swindler.

—Kurt Cobain, *Journals*

The oldest profession assumes many forms, and in Singapore a witty aphorism applies: dirty secrets thrive in clean cities. Or, less whimsically put, "There is a thriving sex business in Singapore. They are just not open about it." That's the observation of Dolly, a former escort agency owner and thirty-year veteran of the trade. "Here in Singapore, you cannot push cards under hotel room doors advertising sex. It's not allowed. If you want to have sex as a customer, you have to do it in a way that is very discreet. It is not advertised except in the *Yellow Pages*."

To understand the high end of the business, she implies, you need to also understand the low end. And to do that, one must confront a paradoxical truism: Escorting is necessarily veiled in secrecy, but low-end sex work is hardly discreet at all.

The most obvious case in point is Orchard Towers, usually the first stop for any newly arrived sex tourist. Affectionately known in local lore as the "four floors" (as in "four floors of whores"), this is an actual shopping center on Orchard Road, located opposite the Singapore Hilton and, incongruously, next to the even more wholesome Palais Renaissance mall with its DKNY Café and upscale boutiques. Orchard Towers really does comprise four floors—of bars and discos, with colorful names like Blue Banana, Green Mango, Peyton Place, Rainforest Club, Ipanema, and Makati City. There's also The Sex Pub, with its tongue-in-cheek sign: "Happy Hours All Night Long."

All night long indeed, working girls openly parade through the premises, moving with brazen impunity in and out of the various bars, many of them decked out in their seductive best. Garments of Lycra and Spandex predominate, exposing as much skin as possible, and some of the more ambitious girls hover outside the entrances, planning to land their catch before he goes inside to ogle the competition. Russian girls proposition customers on the elevator landings, asking S$250 for sex. Cambodian girls openly offer blow jobs for S$100 ("You go toilet, sir? I suck you in toilet for S$100! You like?"). This being Asia, haggling is naturally expected.

Straight guys interested in the Filipinas, Thais, and Indonesians spend evenings at Ipanema or Green Mango. David Brazil, in *No Money, No Honey!*, his 1998 book on the Singapore sex trade, touts Ginivy's Country & Western, the saloon at the building's rear, "a friendly sort of place, with a fairly regular clientele enjoying the live 'Singapore cowboy' music and its female allure." Ginivy's real lure, of course, is never the twangy live band but rather the funky mix of Indonesian, Thai, and Laotian girls.

Then there's the top floor, transformed each evening into a catwalk for the Thai *katoey*, the "ladyboys" primping and preening for the attention of any man in the mood for a gender bender. Real Thai girls, especially the fairer-skinned cream of the crop, hold court in the disco next door, Top Ten. The overall attitude is business-as-usual, and the girls ooze an aura somewhere between audacity and nonchalance. The occasional vice squad raid happens, but they're always arresting poor young things for overstaying their visas, never directly for prostitution. "It's kind of an open secret," admits a former ASP (Assistant Superintendent of Police) who requests anonymity. He had been in a team assigned to study the Orchard Towers phenomenon. "We came to realize that it would be better to leave it the way it is, so that that kind of activity can be centralized."

The other major bastion of centralized sex work is Geylang, an East Coast district known for its legal brothels. The cathouses line the even-numbered streets south of Geylang Road, from Lorong 4 to 24 (The Malay word lorong means "lane"). Most of them are concentrated in a rectangle formed by Geylang Road, Lorong 16, Lorong 20, and Guillemard Road. Each house usually features ten girls and can be identified by colorful numerals sometimes encased in light boxes or by red lanterns hanging outside.

Some houses actually offer a reception service; customers tell the receptionist the type of girl desired and the girl will be called, arriving in under five minutes. The aptly-named Lorong 16, Number 69 is widely considered the best house on that street, perhaps because the adjoining building is designed in the style of a Japanese tea house, filled with spacious bedrooms. Lorong 4 offers pretty Thai girls known for S$40 quickies, sitting "aquarium" style in viewing rooms fitted with plexiglass windows (resembling fish aquariums, for easy selection). By March 2004, however, the specter of urban renewal loomed large: half of Lorong 4 was demolished to accommodate a new freeway, the Kallang/Paya Lebar Expressway, and only one little house (Lorong 4, Number 23) remained open, its eight girls sitting on parade but forcing brave smiles.

According to *Sammy Boy* (*www.sammyboy.com*), the popular online guide to sex work in Singapore, most houses in Geylang operate from 12.30 p.m. to midnight and terms are strictly cash (U.S. dollars are sometimes accepted, seldom at the market rate), with no money-back guarantee. Prices hover around the S$80 to S$100 range, though some houses charge S$150 to S$200 premium rates for better girls, usually those performing massage before and after sex. Geylang girls, as legal sex workers, are also called "yellow card girls" because of their yellow identification cards featuring their photo and thumbprint. These girls undergo medical checkups every two weeks and can work only within the houses. Soliciting openly on the street may result in fines of up to S$1,000 for the first offence, and up to S$2,000 and jail of up to six months, or both, for subsequent offences.

Tipping is optional but very much encouraged if a return visit to the same girl is planned, and payment is usually made not to the girl but to the brothel keeper. "A lot of the brothel keepers are ex-convicts," the former ASP discloses, like a trade secret. "They get licenses to operate as a way for them to make a more decent living, to do something useful in society, and also to keep them from going back to their old ways."

Lesser known, and in danger of extinction, are the other low-end areas like Chinatown's "Blue Triangle" and the Desker Road/Flanders Square enclave tucked inside bustling Little India. The "Blue Triangle," dubbed "the poor man's alternative to Geylang," gets its name from its actual perimeter, the houses being inside a grid formed by three streets (Keong Saik Road, Teck Lim Road, and Jiak Chuan Street). This unique layout was not lost on the Singapore Tourism Board, which now sponsors a walking tour every Friday night called "Secrets of the Red Lantern," with live commentary from a guide who tells enraptured tourists about the women arriving from China in the late 1800s, some 3,000 of them whisked away to service the area's 200 registered brothels.

Today's "Blue Triangle" women are still housed in old, pre-war terraced shophouses, charging anywhere from S$20 (usually a quickie with an older lady) to S$70 or S$100 (for a forty-five-minute session with a girl under 30), with mid-range prices of S$30 to S$50 for thirty minutes with a thirty-something woman. Massage-only services are also available at S$15 a session. Curiously, the women are almost all Chinese, many speaking only dialects like Cantonese or Hokkien, and they don't serve non-Chinese men (or will charge double if they do). Of late, the whole area has been gentrified, offering boutique hotels and fine-dining restaurants, and plans are afoot for all the women to be relocated to Geylang.

Desker Road and Flanders Square are both located in the primarily Indian neighborhood around Serangoon Plaza shopping mall (Desker Road is two blocks south of it, while Flanders Square is one block north). Both places are similar in nature yet different in execution: Desker Road is easily the lowest end of the market, where many sex workers past their prime sit in the front rooms of dingy houses with open doorways, offering sex for as low as S$15. The constant movement of men shuffling up and down the narrow walkways resembles a factory assembly line. Flanders Square is slightly more upmarket, since each girl gets to rent her own room (unlike Desker Road, where the girls often share cubicles), some decorated with Hong Kong movie-star posters and fitted with stereo equipment. Quickies cost

S$30 to S$50, and a full-body massage is S$60 to S$80; full-body treatment means a girl will coat her breasts with scented talc and brush the client's chest with them. Thanks for the mammaries, one might chortle, but if that's too kinky one can opt for a S$15 *bedek bedek* "pretend" massage, ending with a soothing hand job.

Actual massage parlors do exist, all over Singapore, some initially operating in the 1970s as hair salons with secret backrooms furnished with massage beds. Some now prefer to call themselves "health centers," especially if they're located in the Orchard Road malls or in more family-friendly suburbs like Katong. Either way, the going rate is S$50 for masturbation and SS$100 to S$150 for full-on sex. Some offer choices like forty-five-minute massages for S$30 and sixty-minute massages for S$40, excluding tips for the usual extras.

Beyond all this lies the questionably legal realm of the higher classes, like the call girls (strictly defined as those doing only "in-call" work from inside a room or house, with clients secured by phone). In Singapore, most call girls operate out of smaller three-star hotels, charging S$200 or more for 'short-time' sex, their clients arranged by private pimps. In recent years, Russian and other Eastern European girls have occupied this niche, resulting in reports like the one in *The Straits Times* of December 17, 2003, in which one Oysara Yusopova, of Uzbekistan, "who brought in two women to work as prostitutes was jailed for a total of four months and fined S$10,000." Yusopova, forty-one, admitted hiring the girls, aged twenty and twenty-five, and housing them at Hotel Grand Central in Cavanagh Road. The girls met with her in Kuala Lumpur, Malaysia, and were sent down to Singapore, where they made S$7,500 from some twenty to thirty clients from October 3 to October 23, 2003. Anti-vice officers working on a tip-off arrested Yusopova, who couldn't pay the S$10,000 fine and was jailed an extra five weeks in default.

Today, pimps like Yusopova still work girls out of hotels, where they typically charge S$150 to S$200 an hour. Groups of them cruise the corridors of Geylang hotels, and even those in neighboring Joo Chiat, where rooms are S$20 for two hours or S$49 for the whole night. Uzbekistan is actually a fascinating study in the redistribution of wealth; the point of entry is Kuala Lumpur because Malaysia and Uzbekistan are both Muslim countries, which means that the girls can fly out from Tashkent without visas. They hang out in Kuala Lumpur before jetting down to Singapore for bigger profits, since the Singapore dollar's value is usually double the Malaysian *ringgit*.

"But most of them don't speak English well, and also there is quite a high incidence of hepatitis," says Sapphire, the madam of a Singapore escort agency. "I had an Uzbek girl who didn't even know what hepatitis was. When I made her go for a medical check-up, she tested positive for it and I never used her again." For the discerning business traveler, escorts are easily the best option, since quality service means absolute discretion and personal safety. The process of starting an agency is surprisingly easy—a business license to own and operate one can be obtained for S$30 a year, usually renewable every three years, a bargain compared to a S$540-per-year "entertainment license" for running a massage parlor. Escort agencies pay the standard corporate tax, some 20 percent of total profits, and they have to state the total amount earned in commissions by all local escorts (about S$200,000 a year in total, in some cases), who then have to declare and pay income taxes on their own as independent contractors.

Unlike in some parts of the United States, like Utah which has proposed a "sin tax" on escort agencies, there are no additional or special business taxes affecting Singapore escort agencies. They report much like any other business; company directors pay the usual income taxes and claim the usual deductibles on domestic help and child relief. Foreign girls, of course, never appear on any tax paperwork, since they're not legally permitted to work at all. The front desks of some agencies proudly boast photo albums of their girls, all of them Asian faces, but regular clients can dip into other albums kept below the counter featuring blondes and brunettes, available at premium rates for private appointments. Some owners keep no photo albums of girls at all, but can verbally furnish particulars (hair color, country of origin, vital statistics) to clients on request.

While advertising for "escorts" is permissible by law in the *Yellow Pages* but not in the newspapers, classified ads for escorts actually run in *The Straits Times* every week. They always ask for "confidential hostesses" who are "young, pretty, slim, very open-minded," and applicants come in for job interviews, filling in application forms as for any other job. If they're accepted, they'll be briefed about the do's and don'ts of the trade, most of which they'll learn on the job.

When a girl is sent out to meet a client, she is to first ask the client upfront whether he deems her acceptable. If so, she is to call the agency on her cellphone (in industry parlance, to "confirm the job") and then collect the booking fee. Simultaneously, the client submits his wishes for the evening's entertainment. They may go out to dinner or to drink at a karaoke lounge, play pool or attend certain company functions. After the allotted minimum period is over, the man can "extend the booking" and keep the girl longer. The fee for the extension is pro-rated and the girl is tipped for her favors, sexual or otherwise. She keeps the tip but returns the booking fee to the agency, in return for which she may get a cut. Some agencies split the booking fee fifty-fifty if no sex is involved, others work on a sliding-scale incentive program whereby the girl receives a percentage of the booking fee for each repeat customer. In Singapore, there is no single business model and each agency makes its own rules.

The only thing they all share is the facility to "provide companionship," in the words of Terence, an agency owner. "What happens after that has nothing to do with me. By law, we're not supposed to know. We charge a booking fee of so-much, the girl takes so-much, and what they do is their money. I always tell my girls that if there is any sex to be had, the client must ask for it. You are not to be the one who propositions him. This is a dating service, not a fuck shop."

"These are guys who have no time to do the rounds and go pick up girls," he says of his clients. "And they're embarrassed if the girl says no. They want to pick up a nice girl and they don't want to have anything hanging around their necks, especially if they're married." In more poetic terms, "We're doing something immoral for a moral reason," says Cameron, another Singapore agency boss, a former insurance salesman. "Girls come into the business because they have financial problems. They're doing it for a moral reason, to help their families, to support their kids, to settle some disputes. And the men come to me because they're lonely or overstressed." His girls work for no one but him, if they want to work at all. Any girl caught sending private text messages to clients or arranging private appointments is penalized. "I fine them S$50 or S$100. I tell them they are actually stabbing themselves in the back, that they are causing enmity between the trust that is created between them and me."

When a girl comes to Cameron's office for an interview, she has to furnish her particulars on a job application form. One column, entitled "Passable Races," is to be left blank. "That's for my own reference," Cameron explains. "That means I can assess whether the girl looks Chinese or can she pass for something else. This is an acting business. Some girls may be Chinese but can pass for Eurasian, so I tell the customer she's Eurasian. Why not?"

There's always the odd girl out, one who will break his rules and cause him grief. "I sent a girl out for a booking a year or two ago, and she went out for the job and didn't come back," he remembers. "I was waiting for her. I was so angry that I went over to the hotel to get her. I told her she had a responsibility to call back. She said the client didn't want to extend the booking and wanted her to stay on for free! I think she wanted to stay too because they had their own dealings, but anyway I took the girl back. She came back crying. I told her I cared enough for her to personally get her. I was worried about her, I mean who knows what could have happened to her? Some of these girls are walking a fire dance, they don't understand the complexities of the business.

"Like, okay, we keep 40 percent of the fee, that's the market practice, but sometimes their minds are so crazed they want all the money. It really takes work to educate these people. There are a lot of negotiations, like I pay the hotel managers and the doormen, the security people. I pay them a commission—I give them S$30 or S$50—in order to foster a relationship, because they know I have girls who work their hotels." Some security officers, he says, actually stop girls and demand blow jobs in exchange for elevator access. "They victimize these girls," Cameron hisses. "They stop these girls and say, 'You must have 'short-time' with me first.' This is abuse! At some hotels, past a certain time, you have to pay a 'registration fee.' They actually put it on the bill!" Terence and Sapphire both confirm an even more bizarre tactic: some hotel switchboard operators, their palms no doubt well greased, listen in on calls and then tip-off rival agencies, who then send their own girls up to the room. The idea is to persuade the guest to accept the interloper rather than his requested girl. Catfights have resulted in hotel hallways, with girls accusing each other of cutting in on the dance.

This didn't happen in the 1970s, when things were apparently more honest. "I started my agency in 1975," recalls Dolly, who closed it down at the end of 2003, a casualty of the ongoing Singapore recession. "Business was good, much better back then. The men would book the girls to go out for dinner. I had fifty girls back then and it wasn't enough. I would get orders for shipping company parties where I would send twenty girls out all at once. Some of the girls who speak Japanese would escort Japanese gentlemen to play golf. I even had a local girl who could speak Dutch, for the Dutch clients."

"Now, they have KTV bars," she moans. "We didn't have those kinds of places back then. And, that time, it was very cheap. We charged S$120 for four hours, sometimes five hours. Now it's expensive. And there were no Thai women or China women. Back then they would call us up for Singapore girls just through the *Yellow Pages*." The phone book, with its twenty-two pages of escort agencies, has made it "a very visible business," Cameron notes. "The escort market here is actually very centralized. There are only seven or eight real companies, and about six real bosses."

Naturally, Cameron considers himself one of them since he owns several agencies, yet he insists he's not some fat-cat mogul with a money tree in his backyard. "People think this is easy money but it's not. We do more in a day that most people do in a month. Our operation is a complicated one. In one year, I spend half a million dollars on overheads. Phone, salaries, office rentals. S$20,000 a year on my phone lines. S$140,000 a year on advertising. I need S$30,000 income each month to cover my costs."

So why should anyone use an escort agency when any

hot-blooded male can pick up a girl at Orchard Towers, where concepts like booking fees don't apply? Well, Cameron explains, a good agency indemnifies the client from unfortunate events. He can call the agency if the girl steals a client's wallet or fails to provide adequate service. "At one of the more prestigious hotels, about a year ago, a guest picked up a girl off the street," Cameron recalls. "She spiked his drink, and he lost about S$15,000."

Also, the guy minimizes his chances of contracting a sexually transmitted disease. "I expect to see the girls' HIV reports, all their medical reports, or else they're out of the business," Cameron says. "The way the medical thing works is, I have a doctor who understands the nature of the business and my girls go to him for their own checkups. I don't pay for them, the girls have to pay themselves. But they're monitored. They can go to their own doctor, or any doctor, if they like, but I tell them if they don't show me their reports, they don't work."

During the 1970s, the better agencies even scheduled etiquette classes. Girls were taught how to dress, how to walk, how to talk. Quality control was critical, since there might be fifty or one hundred and fifty girls working at any given agency, many of them flying the Asia-Pacific region on high-turnaround trysts. One agency habitually flew in girls from Europe and sent them out from Singapore, to rich clients in Malaysia, Indonesia, and Hong Kong. A *Playboy* centerfold did this at a rate of S$6,000 a night, and a British girl based in Hong Kong did the same. Then there was an Asian businessman who liked white girls, so two of them flew in to Paris, one from Miami and the other from Prague, and checked into the same hotel, his room number already provided by the agency in Singapore. The same agency also arranged for eight girls, all from different countries, to fly to Australia for a group of wealthy Asian executives, entertaining them in Sydney, Melbourne, and Perth.

And then, there was a little speck on the map called Brunei.

The oil-rich kingdom, nestled between the East Malaysian states of Sabah and Sarawak, has earned its place in sex business folklore. In the 1980s, many an escort would return from Brunei well compensated, with wild stories to tell. "In those days, ten years ago, I would send ten girls to Brunei, all at once," Dolly remembers. "They paid my ladies S$10,000 each, a lot of money. I hear the ones who are lucky get S$10,000 and the ones who are not so lucky—sometimes they decide they don't want certain girls and send them back to Singapore—those girls still get S$2,000 each." In 1997, however, beauty queen Shannon Marketic, twenty-seven, the 1992 Miss U.S.A., sued Prince Jefri Bolkiah, forty-four, youngest brother of the Sultan of Brunei, for US$90 million. Marketic alleged that that she and six other women were held captive in Brunei for thirty-two days, for the express purpose of sex. ("Prince Removed From Sex-Slave Suit," proclaimed the *Associated Press* headline of March 6, 1998, after a U.S. district judge ruled that Prince Jefri was covered under the Foreign Sovereign Immunity Act, which protected him from litigation in the United States).

Meantime, allegations arose that Prince Jefri had stashed prostitutes in his US$21-million home in the posh Park Lane district of London; writer Michael Horsnell, of *The Times* of London, reported on the prince's lavish lifestyle, observing that he owned a US$5-million set of ten gold watches displaying mechanically-copulating couples. In 2001, the sexually voracious prince was banished from Brunei after apparently embezzling some US$15 billion from his own government, and he fled into exile in Paris and London.

Gone he may have been but not forgotten. Sex workers in the United States still sigh whenever the subject of Brunei comes up: strippers in New Orleans flown out to Brunei simply to adorn parties; porn stars returned and supplemented their income by recommending other girls; one adult film star bragged about the time she went to Brunei only to be told that there were too many girls, so they sent her home—after paying her a kill fee of, US$20,000. "Should you actually sleep with someone," she cooed to another girl back in Los Angeles, "you'll get a hundred thousand dollars." The girl, wide-eyed and slack-jawed, agreed to go. The bearer of glad tidings beamed, having just earned her finder's fee.

"They'll give you a briefcase full of money and you get jewelry and Rolexes and any branded things you want," says Sapphire, who also sent girls to Brunei. "When you're leaving, you'll get people carrying your briefcase, straight to the flight. If the guy really likes you, he will call you directly for another trip. Some of them will give the girls money to buy houses and cars in their home countries." In October 2003, Sapphire sent a pretty young girl from Colombia. "They booked her as a present, to seal a business deal."

But who is "they," one is prompted to ask, and how does it really work? "Brunei is always done through a third party," Sapphire explains. "I will get calls from people who know people in Brunei, who are entertaining them directly."

These intermediaries, who pay her for the job (never the men who actually receive the girls), are often business associates from prominent firms or multinational conglomerates based in Singapore. "These days, when a third party takes one of my girls, they will offer S$10,000. But I know that actually they're getting paid S$20,000. So I will usually say to the girl, okay, I'll take S$3,000 and you take S$7,000." This split is for "hostessing"—straight escorting with no sex, whereby the S$3,000 is the *de facto* booking fee.

If sex is involved, the girl splits her tip fifty-fifty with Sapphire. "When the girls go there, they have to dress up for the evening. By six o'clock, they have to be dressed elegantly and then go out to karaoke and disco, and there's food and everything there. Just look pretty and be there, that's all they really have to do. And then, if anyone wants to dance or sing with them, or invite them, then that's extra tip for them." Regular clients also book girls to accompany them overseas, to exotic destinations like Bali and Phuket. In such cases, "the client has to transmit the money and the airfare into my account first. He has to pay upfront."

"I once sent two girls to Indonesia, for a very big party," Sapphire recalls. "They wanted European girls, for a certain number of days. I said they would have to pay S$2,000 per day. They took the girls for five days. So that was S$10,000 each girl, plus they had to pay for airfare and arrange the girls' accommodation, food, lodging, everything. Once they remitted the money to my account, I would arrange for the girls to fly out on that day. The money the girls get is split fifty-fifty with me."

Today, Sapphire takes serious umbrage with the "China girls," the China-born women found mostly in massage parlors and KTV bars. Some even boldly streetwalk in Geylang, tramping on the turf of the legal brothels. "I've used China girls before. They're hopeless. They want a lot of money but they're so cold. Sexually cold. They're like a log of wood. My customers tell me they can book other girls twice for the same amount of money and get better service. Plus they can't speak English very well, so I can't talk to them about what I need them to do. So they just do as they like. Sometimes, they'll use the customer's hotel phone to call overseas. One time, this girl went to the toilet and used the phone there—to call China! The customer complained, but only much later. If I had known, I would have docked her money and paid the guy something back for his phone bill."

Dolly laments the same: "A lot of the mainland Chinese girls are not honest. You give them the bookings but now they have their own phones and pagers, and so they can do their own business. Often they would go for the job and then not come back to pay you. This kept happening from about two years ago, and we were losing money. I knew my business was in trouble when a number of these girls, who were students here wanting to earn extra money, actually told me they could go out on their own and get men." In late 2003, the Singapore government, taking the moral high ground as usual, acted to restrict the work visas of the *pei du mama*, the Chinese women who move to Singapore to accompany their children studying here, paying the bills through sex work. They are no longer allowed to work in their first year in Singapore.

Some agencies reported that business plummeted some 50 percent in 2003, blaming it on the ongoing impact of the recession and the March SARS outbreak which almost destroyed the Southeast Asian travel industry. With everyone's resources stretched thinner, the usually affable clients became harder to please. "I would say that there are only a handful of clients now who will bother to take the girl out to dinner first," Terence sighs. "People's attitudes have changed. Before, the girls would be tipped S$200 or S$300 and it was all nice and fun, without even having to do anything extra. Today it's different. The clients expect to have sex."

Things usually work in favor of the local girls, though. Terence notices that his clients who need regular girls seldom pick foreigners. "I had a Colombian girl who told me she thought that the maximum number of trips a foreign girl should make to Singapore is three," he says. "I think she's right. The best anyone has done here is four. The clients like to switch around, try different girls each time." Caucasian women are considered novelties, short-term spending, there to fulfill some notions of sexual exotica. Happy endings are rare but sometimes do happen: one of Terence's Eastern European girls actually married a client, a wealthy local businessman, and today they still live in a nice, suburban part of Singapore, all ties to her past disavowed.

Dolly remembers that some of her girls married European clients and relocated. "One of them is now a nurse in London. Her English wasn't very good but she studied and got better. They came to visit me recently. The husband thanked me for introducing me to his wife. He said, 'If you didn't have your agency, I wouldn't have met my wife!' He was very proud. 'Yes, my wife was an escort but she is a very nice woman.' So, out of ten men, I will get one like him, who will say that not all escorts are bad girls."

Cameron, however, is a cynic when romance enters the equation. "Some of these girls come back when their husbands leave them," he says. "And I laugh at them. I always tell them: 'Never marry your client. Never cohabit.' Why? Firstly, they call an escort and pay thousands of dollars every month, but if you become a wife or a lover, they can have you as many times as they like and you cannot say no. You're obligated. So, if you leave my company, go out the door and never come back. I don't want you. Get away from me. You don't appreciate kindness and you've taken me for granted. You're just an opportunist."

Curiously, he himself is married to a former escort, a girl from Manila who'd serviced the U.S. servicemen at Clark Air Base. He also owns a number of escorting websites, all listing prices for several options, from "female companionship" to "evening escorts," and insists there's nothing wrong with that. "You can use the term 'discreet services' in the *Yellow Pages*, so why can't I do the same on the Internet?" he argues. "Yes, on my sites, 'sensual companionship' is S$300 per hour. But that could be anything."

Terence disagrees. His own company website lists no

prices whatsoever, and anyone desiring his escorts has to email or call him for further inquiry. This is how it should work, every transaction discreetly done, and he says he speaks for all the agency owners concerning the "many levels of misconception and misunderstanding," some of it stemming from a mid-1980s fiasco—five girls were sent out to a ship, an oil tanker, and were never seen again. The case remains unsolved.

"They were called escorts in the newspapers, but they were not escorts!" he bellows. "They were girls working out of an apartment on Clemenceau Avenue, being pimped by a lady who owned the place. The same kinds of girls are doing 'short-time' work out of small hotels today. These girls are not escorts. The whole thing has given our business a bad name."

Cameron's websites with their comparison-shopping fees, he sneers, sets an unwelcome precedent. Escorting, unlike other areas of the flesh trade, is a much kinder, more genteel business. "To openly put a price on a woman, I actually find that distasteful," he says. "Anything beyond escorting is a personal thing to both of them. I'm not marketing sex."

Daughters Of The Tenth Muse

I feel five hundred years old, but I keep
in mind that I am never too old to learn.

— Heidi Fleiss, *Pandering*

When an escort agency owner claims he's not
marketing sex, he's unwittingly fallen into the abyss
of euphemism. Once the booking fee is agreed upon and
money changes hands, what else, really, is supposed to
happen after dinner?

Escorts are sex surrogates with excellent social skills,
unlike girls in a brothel who aren't expected to talk at all.
Theirs is a tradition descended from the ancient Greeks. The
highest class of prostitutes were the *hetaerae*, a class of
educated women who were companions for the Athenian
male elite. Male misogyny actually created the *hetaerae*.
Athenian culture dictated that women were not allowed to
be educated and, once married, were required to stay home,

isolated from the outside world. So the men sought women more interesting than their wives, female companions adept at the art of conversation. Lo, like a thunderbolt from Zeus, the escorting profession was born!

Sometimes, the *hetaerae* were young boys (hence the slang term "Greek" for anal sex), but regardless of gender they were different from the *porne*—the ordinary, garden-variety prostitutes, from which is derived the modern word "pornography," from *porne* (prostitute) and *graphien* (writing). The *hetaerae* did not usually accept cash but instead preferred gifts in exchange for their services.

Sappho, the most famous of the *hetaerae*, whom Plato called "the tenth muse," left a profound legacy: her love for the women of the island of Lesbos, around 600 BC, resulted in the modern term "lesbian." Her descendents have sprinkled their lust dust through the ages. In the early days of San Francisco, prostitutes were called Cyprians, after the island of Cyprus, center of worship for the love goddess Aphrodite. Artists have always used them as muses—the painter Toulouse-Lautrec in the salons and streets of Paris, the photographer F.J. Belloq in the red-light Storyville district of New Orleans, today's filmmakers in their celluloid shrines (Catherine Deneuve in *Belle du Jour*, Jane Fonda in

Klute, Julia Roberts in *Pretty Woman*, Rebecca De Mornay in *Risky Business*, Jodie Foster in *Taxi Driver*, Brooke Shields and Susan Sarandon in *Pretty Baby*, even Blondie's Debbie Harry as a madam in the HBO movie *Confessions of Beverly Hills*). Eloquently humanized, they've seeped their way into the modern consciousness.

In Asia, however, little exaltation has taken place, despite the long history of Asian erotica, from the legendary Indian *kama sutra* to the tales of Chinese concubines. The most noteworthy cultural event about Asian sex workers in 2003 actually took place in San Francisco and New York, a photography exhibit by a fifth-generation Chinese-American, Reagan Louie. His *Sex Work in Asia* show is also available in book form, a 192-page book called *Orientalia: Sex in Asia*, published in September 2003. Louie shot his girls in the bars and brothels of Seoul, Tokyo, Bangkok, Hong Kong, and even Guangdong province in southern China. "Beautiful pictures," Sandra Philips, the San Francisco Museum of Art's photography curator, described them to *The New York Times*, "very allusive and colorful, layered, resonant, not easy, and certainly thoughtful and humane."

But why has the thoughtful and humane found a more

comfortable home in the West, when the source matter is unequivocally Asian? Perhaps it's because the subject matter is still largely debased and vilified on its home soil. Louie, ambitiously, noted that he aimed to dispel Western stereotypes and myths about "exotic" Asian women. Yet in Asia, those stereotypes and myths are actually promoted, even distorted, through the prism of what passes for public knowledge. Commercial sex, to most Asians, means vice squad raids as reported in the Asian newspapers. It means photos of ashen-faced, dusky-skinned nymphs bowing their heads in shame, led away by poker-faced undercover policemen.

The stories are many, all variations on a single theme.

On a single day in January of 2004, more than one hundred girls from China, Vietnam, and the Philippines were arrested in Singapore, a whopping sixty of them at the infamous Paramount Shopping Centre in Katong and others at the Blue Star Pub in Joo Chiat. "We started the raids at about 10 p.m.," a police inspector told *The Straits Times*. "This was one of our routine raids to check on those who are working here illegally, or those who are involved in illegal activities."

On October 28, 2003, Hong Kong police arrested

233 women in Kowloon West, after a pre-dawn sweep of fifty-two locations. Most of the girls came from Thailand and mainland China. In the first nine months of 2003, the *Hongkong Standard* reported, some 12,000 mainland Chinese had been arrested, compared to 11,717 for the whole of 2002. Nury Vittachi and Kate Whitehead, in their 1997 book *After Suzie: Sex in South China*, noted that "prostitution is legal in Hong Kong but everything associated with it, such as soliciting, pimping or living off the earnings of a prostitute, is illegal"; yet British babes continue to flourish as escorts ("because hotel security never stop Western women") and Chinese men can sit in those dark places the locals dub "fishball stalls" (where, for a paltry HK$180 (US$30), a girl will simulate for his genitals "the rubbing and squeezing motion used by the Chinese in making fishballs, small globes of minced fish and spices").

In early February 2004, a girl from the fundamentalist Muslim state of Kelantan in Malaysia was arrested for working as a call girl, earning RM150 (S$66) per session from a hotel room on the holiday island of Penang. Scandalously, she was a university student on a government scholarship ("Call Girl a Govt Scholar," ran one headline, and *The Malay Mail* cited a source saying, "The girl did not have any financial worries regarding her education. As such it is puzzling why she resorted to such activities"). Lawmakers in Kuala Lumpur were behooved to care, because she was arrested along with another girl, a graduate from a university in the capital state of Selangor.

In Bangkok, new laws have crippled the sex scene. Live sex shows are now banned. Effective March 1, 2004, all girlie bars may only open at 9 p.m. and must close by midnight, instead of the usual 4 a.m. Bars in three areas—Patpong, Ratchadapisek, and Rama IX—are partially exempted, their new closing time being 2 a.m. Such are the social reforms proposed by Thai Deputy Prime Minister Purachai Piemsombun ("who should move into a monastery, according to one indignant club owner," reported *The Straits Times* on February 15, 2004). Cooks and waiters are being laid-off in light of the new hours, and takings have already fallen by as much as 50 percent in most places, where the action on any given night doesn't ever start before midnight anyway. Contrary to popular belief, prostitution is actually illegal in Thailand—perhaps a surprising fact in a country where, as Thai Member of Parliament, Suchart Bandasak, pointedly reminded everyone, "It is a man's personal right to visit massage parlors or have more than one wife."

But personal rights are debatable throughout Asia, especially where sex is concerned. Law enforcement generally works at the expense of sex workers, and public censure imposes on them a sense of shame, forcing them to constantly question their self-identity. Business opportunities wrestle with personal values, all very aptly yin and yang, and so the agency owner who insists he's "not marketing sex" is speaking the same language as the KTV hostess who says she's merely a "high-class waitress." Emily, a Singaporean Chinese escort, maintains that such distinctions are ludicrous. "These KTV girls strip half-naked in the rooms," she says, "and if the customers can afford them, they will have sex. The way they look, the way they dress, one look and you can tell they're KTV girls but, really, it's like being a hooker. If you can take off your clothes so easily, then what's so special about you? Nothing. What's so great about taking off your clothes in public? If you want to get intimate with someone, don't you think it should be done in a room where people are not looking, rather than in a place where people are high or drunk?"

Emily's approach is almost coldly mathematical, since she believes that escorting offers elegant solutions to practical problems. "I think that if you're escorting, you should behave yourself," she declares. "There are rules to be observed. I respect myself and I respect my customers and I don't behave like a prostitute. I behave like his friend." However, she's an expensive friend to have, a local girl who's worked in Bali and Brunei, with a resume parallel to those of the European models and *Playboy* Playmates who consort with Arab sheiks in Paris, as documented in countless magazines.

American porn stars who turn tricks are always in circulation, like the greenbacks they earn. "I don't know the exact numbers but I can tell you it's pretty high," says retired porn star Melissa Monet, the star of such X-rated epics as *Whispered Secrets of the Call Girls*, *Sodomania 11*, and *Dangerous Rapture*. A former escort-turned-madam, she operated out of both her native New York and her adopted Los Angeles. "Desperation is a great motivator. Most of the girls get into it after they've had their run making movies or at least near the very end. They find it easier than lowering their rates and losing face, so to speak, by doing gangbangs for half what their rate was to do a simple boy/girl scene.

"Most of these girls come into the sex industry with no real life experience, and they learn about sex and about who they are from a very narrow point of view. How can anyone expect them to have self-esteem? They've never been anything but a whore, first to please their families and now to please men.

"I never lied to myself while I was working," Melissa adds. "When my best friend and I got together to truly discuss it, we always admitted that we were just hookers with knowledge of Masters and Johnson techniques. When we became call girls, that's what we called ourselves. There is a difference, if ever so slight, since a hooker has to physically solicit whereas a call girl advertises. Even drug dealers have their hierarchy, so why shouldn't the girls? When I was a madam, I was just that, although, because of the prices I charged and the prices the girls received, they could indeed call themselves high-class call girls. But I truly believe that if a girl has to put a label on something to justify what she's doing, she's in the wrong business."

Melissa is among the rare few who has found perverse pleasure in her profession, to the point of epiphany. "It takes confidence to be a great whore," she declares. "Look at the courtesans of old. Those women had it all! Unfortunately, the difference today is in the way society looks upon us. We are still desired by all, yet repulsed by the masses." The chasm is so wide, but that's precisely why Melissa emphasizes the idea of self-confidence. A sex worker's sanity hinges precariously on her metaphysical boundaries. As former stripper Lily Burana, in her autobiography *Strip City*, reflects: "Stripping takes out of me things that I didn't even realize I had. The near-nudity isn't the problem, or the physical vulnerability, or working well outside the margins of acceptable female behavior. It's the damn neediness: Angry men scowling at me like they can buy me for a dollar, lonely men professing love after a ten-minute chat with the specter of femininity that wafts before them, and confused and desperate men convinced that if only they could get a girl to do what they ask, however outlandish, things will be better somehow.

"These men don't just hunger for a glimpse of skin, because they could stay home and look at Miss August were that the case. They want some kind of connection, to tap the life of a live, nude girl. And no amount of professional distance on my part can keep that leeching feeling at bay."

Her words repudiate all the easy jibes about sex work, the kind of stuff that sells men's magazines ("*Can't find a nice girl? Rent a bad one*"), and raises the bar for escorts who need professional distance. A client will wine and dine an escort, but both already know how the evening is supposed to end, so how should one resolve this existential conundrum? "When a man looks at a women and sees only somebody to go to bed with," suggests the mythology scholar Joseph Campbell, "he is seeing her in relation to a fulfillment of some need of his own and not as a woman at all. It's like looking at cows and thinking only of roast beef."

Some have profited from this basic instinct, despite the odd jail term or two, since they've fed bestsellers to a public hungry for titillation. They've written about their own lives in sex work: Xaviera Hollander, author of *The Happy Hooker*; Sidney Biddle Barrows, author of *Mayflower Madam*; and Heidi Fleiss, author of *Pandering*. Even male escorts are now playing the game, notably David Henry Sterry, author of *Chicken: Love for Sale on the Streets of Hollywood* and Aaron Lawrence, author of *Suburban Hustler: Stories of a Hi-Tech Callboy*. In Asia, Chinese author Jiu Dan published her 2001 novel *Wuya* (*Crows*), a controversial novel about the *xiolongnu* ("little dragon girls"), the girls from China who work as prostitutes in Singapore. It fetched US$500,000 (S$930,000) for the U.S. movie rights, and she was last reported asking HK$1 million (S$239,000) for the Hong Kong film rights. However, she forbade the release in Singapore of her follow-up book,

Lovers of Singapore, to "avoid unnecessary speculations" about her own kiss-and-tell exploits with Singapore men.

Christine, twenty-two, a Chinese girl from Kota Kinabalu in East Malaysia, could have written that book, too. Having left a S$2,000-a-month job as a bar girl to move to Singapore, where she now works full-time in a Katong massage parlor, she doesn't pretend to be like the KTV girls. "Am I a prostitute?" she ponders, for all of two seconds. "Yes. I admit it. I'm okay with that. It's money that I've earned myself. I don't steal and I don't cheat. This is what I exchange, to make a living. I accept what I do."

"Some girls don't want to have to reveal themselves in this way or they're embarrassed about it," she shrugs. "But if you don't take it to heart, it's okay. It doesn't bother me when people talk bad about me. You can't do this kind of work if you have to think about what other people will say." The job actually comes with some severe costs. According to Florence, the affable, middle-aged massage parlor owner, Christine has to forfeit S$240 each month towards her CPF (Central Provident Fund, Singapore's mandatory social security savings scheme), since she didn't make it past Form 5 (7th Grade in the United States). Malaysians educated at Form 5 or higher pay only S$30 per month. Florence pays

S$540 each year for her "entertainment license," a startling difference from an escort agency's dues (S$30 a year or S$75 for a three-year business license). The rationale is that escort agencies do not transact business on their premises, whereas massage parlors do. What happens behind closed doors matters after all.

Had Christine chosen to become an escort or a KTV hostess, she might not be so honest about her self-identity. Massage girls aren't afforded the built-in facade of companionship (as escorts are) or waitressing (as KTV hostesses are), so there's no place left for her to rationalize her livelihood. Yet her harder-edged reality is something she cherishes. She's literally, and figuratively, naked all the time, kept in touch with her sense of self. "I know that I can attract men sexually," Christine offers. "I knew that from working at the pub, where men would approach me for sex. I know I am good at talking to the customers, at saying things to seduce them. I have had sex with them for money, but only with the good customers, the ones I knew well or felt comfortable with. I did it because I had financial problems with my family and also because I like sex. I'm very frank about that."

Christine worked the bar for two years and quit, then

tried being a hairdresser before succumbing to family pressure. Her father is a truck driver, her mother a seamstress, and she has four other siblings to help feed. "They don't know I am here doing this," she confesses. "I told them I am still working in a bar. They would be upset if they knew the truth. Can you imagine? I even had one guy who wanted to lick my feet and suck my toes. No sex. He tipped me S$50, to let him suck my toes! How would they react to that?"

An escort might earn S$500 for the same, but then is money the only difference? Surely there's some vulnerability involved in offering your digits for inspection and lubrication. Sociologist Kimberly-Anne Ford, from Concordia University in Montreal, Canada, considers sex work a legitimate form of social work, having done studies "evaluating prostitution as a human-service occupation." She cites social theorist Charles Taylor's position, that "our identity is partly shaped by recognition or its absence...and so a person or a group of people can suffer real damage or real distortion if the people or society around them mirror back to them a confining or demeaning or contemptible picture of themselves."

The same point is driven home by Harvard Medical

School researcher Alexa Albert in her book, *Brothel: Mustang Ranch and Its Women*, about the legal whorehouses of Nevada. "Consensual sex between adults—whether for pay or *pro bono*—is exactly that, consensual," Albert urges. "As such, it's a personal and private decision. What seems universally to be true about it is our need to supercharge it politically and load it down with the heavy freight of moral issues."

To be an escort is to disregard that load, preferring an outlook that's almost too sanguine. "I think most people say business and pleasure are separate, but I can't seem to do that," says Melanie, from New Zealand, who has worked Orchard Road hotel rooms with the same Singapore agency since 1997. "I try to bring as much pleasure to business, so that it then becomes more enjoyable. Then it's just like having a job or having a career, where if you succeed then your life means something more."

Melanie acquired a deliciously clipped accent from four years of living in England, and she resembles the sultry actress Jessica Alba from the television series *Dark Angel*—she's the semi-Caucasian/semi-something-else type now dubbed EA, ("ethnically ambiguous"), a modern marketer's wet dream. She can wax nostalgic about her earlier years in

Singapore. "We'd have like fifteen girls and organize parties. We'd serve tea and the girls wouldn't have to sleep with anybody, and it was fun. Now, you don't even have a meeting and you have to go straight up to the hotel to meet a total stranger. You never get used to it. You can get a situation where the guy gets worried that he won't have enough time with you and he has only half an hour till two o'clock in the morning and you then get asked to give a discount. And that's when I go, 'Excuse me?!'

"I want guys who want to know me as a person, where you know you can have a good time instead of, 'I don't care who you are or what you're about, all I'm interested in is this.' Okay, fine, yes, you can have that, too. But I don't want just that. I want them to just chill out. I prefer guys who can have fun. Some girls don't like that, they think it's too much work and it gets too personal. They do see it as work. They're not really interested in them as people."

Melanie's need for empathy probably comes from being a voracious reader. Each trip to Singapore includes a visit to her favorite bookstore, Kinokuniya in the Ngee Ann City mall, where she spends hundreds of dollars each time. "I've read Xaviera Hollander's *The Happy Hooker* and now I'd like Margaret MacDonald to write a book," she enthuses, referring to the forty-four-year-old English madam arrested in September 2003 for running an "elite international prostitution ring," as the Reuters wire story called it. Based in Paris, MacDonald spoke ten languages, carried four cellphones, and deployed an awesome force of 538 girls working from yachts anchored off the Côte d'Azur and luxury hotels across Europe, charging 1000 euros (S$1,980) an hour. She received four years' jail and a fine of 150,000 euros, but that's not the point. "I want her to write something about it because she's a normal person," Melanie says, "in the same way that I'd consider myself a normal person."

By that, she implies a longing for social acceptance, for the way the ancient Greeks accepted the *hetaerae*. It's not an easy thing to come by, especially in Asia, where some of the things she does are certainly never discussed in polite company. But when work means sodomizing a cross-dresser with a dildo or spanking a foot-fetish client with her stiletto heels, what part of herself can she hold on to like a touchstone, a reminder that she is a "normal person"?

The answer lies in a deceptively simple idea. Sappho was a poet, after all, and all good escorts are expected to live by this dictum: good conversation is foreplay.

The quality of an escort's social skills determines her value, expresses her essence, and defines her identity. In a world where all women are roast beef to the carnally carnivorous, any beautiful woman can step out of a designer dress wearing only a shimmering pendant and a persuasive smile. But a good escort knows how to keep a man interested for the first three hours, before her baser instincts kick in to keep him aroused during the last. She knows when to loosen that shoulder strap, when to allow him to caress her smooth skin and taste her nether regions, when to produce paroxysms of delight to remind him of the dance of desire.

And when to say goodbye, for her next appointment is waiting. Her time is always expensive. And always running out.

Invisible Trade

> For me, sex is the most interesting area of our
> lives. It is a source of ecstasy, pain, discovery
> and inspiration. It's a space where we can
> connect, learn about others and ourselves;
> where we hope, where we heal. It can be a
> microcosm of life itself, a minidrama of politics,
> identity, and power.
>
> — Tristan Taormino, *Tristan Taormino's True Lust*

Jasmine checks her watch and smiles. Only 9.30 p.m.;
Philip made good time. She didn't even know he was
coming when she had his neck clasped between her thighs,
but she enjoyed watching him reach his usual quick climax.
She knew when he stopped tensing up and his body
suddenly relaxed.

Jasmine finds herself lost in thought as she waltzes out of
the hotel. The twenty-minute taxi ride back to her apartment
offers time to rest and reflect. Last week, a client brought her

roses, with a ring inside. She thinks marriage proposals are flattering but absurd. As Heidi Fleiss liked to remind her girls, escorting is "a stepping-stone, not a career." Before her conviction in December 1994, Heidi's life was driven by one thing: the relentless pursuit of "the 40 percent"—her commission. This meant an escort's life was about the remaining 60 percent, the amount that each girl kept.

Well, Jasmine thinks, that's a new spin on the old idea of being a kept woman. Of course, she's never going to accept a marriage proposal from a client. That would get in the way of her life, liberty and the pursuit of the next 60 percent.

Right now, though, Jasmine was in a good place. She'd made a very nice chunk of change to take home to Ulan Bator and had Singapore to thank for it. If it hadn't been such a transient place, full of rich foreigners passing through, like all the American and European men making pit-stops en route to Australia or elsewhere in Asia, she wouldn't have had clients. It was curious how none of the books or articles she'd read about escorting, or even sex work in general, said much about Singapore. Bangkok had Patpong and Pattaya, and the infinitely more exotic Soi Cowboy off Sukhumvit Road. Tokyo had Roppongi with its conveyor-belt sushi girls.

And Jakarta, man, Jakarta was abuzz with places like Tanah Abang where the girls outnumbered men by nine to one. These are "rent girls," as Karl Taro Greenfeld observes in his book of Asian memoirs, *Standard Deviations*, "to be taken home and banged silly." The sex industry in Indonesia rakes in US$3.3 billion (S$5.7 billion) a year, a whole two percent of the country's gross domestic product, rather impressive for a supposedly underground industry.

Singapore's place in the sex worker universe was secured by *Saint Jack*, the Paul Theroux novel published in 1973, which director Peter Bogdanovich filmed on location in 1978. The movie, originally entitled *Jack of Hearts*, stars Ben Gazzara as an American pimp in Singapore and it was banned for seventeen years. The Singapore Board of Film Censors viewed it and "were aghast at its portrayal of Singapore as a seedy fleshpot of a country, rife with gangsters, pimps and prostitutes," noted *The Straits Times* of January 24, 1980. (The film's status in Singapore is presently uncertain, in light of a new film rating system, introduced in March 2004.)

The Singapore International Film Festival's organizers pleaded the case for the film as an important document of early-70s Singapore, with its striking shots of the Singapore

195

River and its *tongkang* boats, the riverside *godowns* of Boat Quay, the old Chinatown with its colorful streets and even more colorful gangsters cussing in Hokkien dialect, which Bogdanovich left intact in the finished film.

It was finally shown at the festival in 1997, but only once. ("To discourage interest, the film was screened at a late and unsocial hour for the early-to-bed Singaporeans," a bemused Theroux told the *South China Morning Post*). The film's multi-national cast included a beautiful Singaporean Indian actress named Monika Subramaniam, who became Bogdanovich's sometime squeeze—an affair later exposed with some bile in *Cybill Disobedience*, the autobiography of his then-girlfriend, actress Cybill Shepherd. *Saint Jack* remains Subramaniam's sole claim to fame, and she was clearly written into the script (since her character does not exist in Theroux's book), to cleverly illustrate the country's multi-racial mix, the heady melting pot where Jasmine derives her clients.

The multitude of cultural differences certainly offers variety to spice up her life, especially since one out of every four persons living in Singapore today is a foreigner. "I like the Caucasian guys better than the local or Chinese guys, because I would say they are more open-minded and better communicators than Asian guys," explains Jasmine. "Japanese men are interesting, but the Europeans are the ones who like weird things. like strangulation and fantasies. By fantasies, I mean they want me to dress in a specific way, like a schoolgirl or in normal skirts but with no underwear. The Singaporean guys are really terrible. I have no idea why. When it comes to sex, they tend to be a bit rough or they don't really know what to do sexually. I think it has to do with the way they grew up. It's probably the environment."

Small wonder, that Singapore finished last again in the Durex international sex survey, for the second straight year. Singaporeans aren't enthusiastic about sex, six times a month being the maximum desired frequency. The average Singaporean has sex ninety-six times a year, compared to the global average of 127. Yet 71 percent say they're happy with their sex lives and only 18 percent admit to having paid for sex.

All this takes place in the environment Jasmine alludes to, where oral sex between consenting adults is illegal (thanks to an archaic law from the British colonial days), where the television series *Sex & the City* is still not shown and tame men's magazines like *Playboy* still cannot be sold. Even the barely racy women's magazine *Cosmopolitan* was actually banned in Singapore for a whole twenty years, until it was "degazetted" by the government's media watchdog unit, the Media Development Authority, in September 2003.

The latest furor in the press concerned parents getting upset when their kids were caught with pornographic VCDs. Should anyone be surprised? Forbidden fruit must taste sweeter to impressionable youngsters, since pornography is banned. Singaporeans are "a people under constant surveillance, whether from the authorities, family, work or the expectations of a rigid society," says Colin Goh, editor of the satirical website *Talking Cock* (*www.talkingcock.com*), in a *Straits Times* opinion column.

He was reacting to the latest minidrama, already the subject of ridicule in many foreign newspapers: the country's low birthrate problem was going to be solved with a year-long "Romancing Singapore" festival, which encouraged singles to date more with the help of a booklet called *When Boy Meets Girl: The Chemistry Guide*, issued by the government. Surely no more ludicrous situation exists than a country where its citizens have to taught how to date! "We're unromantic because we have little space to be ourselves," Goh wrote. "Romance is personal, spontaneous, clandestine, intimate. It comprises shared confidences, private utterances, bared vulnerabilities. It's conducted in shadows, not in fluorescent-lit rooms filled with fluffy bears, plastic hearts, Celine Dion muzak, and especially other people."

All this does is further solidify Singapore's reputation as the "Nanny State of Asia" (a hilarious sobriquet supplanting William Gibson's more famous but grim "Disneyland with the Death Penalty"). Poor Austin Powers nearly lost his *mojo* when the Singapore censors clumsily tried to repackage *The Spy Who Shagged Me* as *The Spy Who Shioked Me* ("*shiok*" being the local Singlish patois for "pleasurable"). Yet Jasmine's *mojo* is always working, because escorting "is legal here," according to a former police superintendent. "It's a way of ensuring demand and supply. The agency owner is not strictly a pimp, he doesn't make any deals about sex. That's between the customer and the girl. This is the high end of the business. Any situation where the girl makes S$400 or more is considered high-class here."

What most people know about the international sex business is that some 700,000 women are trafficked globally each year, as a *New York Times* article estimates. But most of these women are not of Jasmine's pedigree. They include the poor Cambodian girls hailing from the hovels of

Pailin and Poipet, eking a very modest living in the brothels of Southeast Asia. They only see the inside of a five-star hotel by following a john back to his suite, after settling on the price at the bar. Jasmine gets to go directly to the suite, to entertain kinky English guys like Philip, who pays S$600 to get strangled. Other guys fork out S$700 to S$1,000 an hour, for sex with some spanking or whipping. These are the dangerous liaisons she lives for, challenging the frontiers of sexual behavior, in a country known for imposing sexual convention.

It's an ironic situation, if not an entirely romantic one, but it sure is personal, spontaneous, clandestine, and intimate. "Nightlife in Singapore is like having a party with your parents in the house," William Moss, an American expatriate, told the *International Herald Tribune* in 2003. He clearly hadn't met the likes of Jasmine, who has already coerced the parents into the basement, slammed the trapdoor shut and thrown away the key.

The party continues unabated, but behind closed doors. The secrecy is what makes it so sexy, Jasmine realizes, as she gets out of the cab and unlocks her front door. On any given evening, a hotel rendezvous will be known to only three people: her madam, her client, and herself. Hers is an alternative reality, a world where she's only available to those who know.

Those who know, because they have the money, to gain access to this invisible trade.

Acknowledgments

In the whirlwind six months taken to research this book, numerous people were helpful and I would like to thank them as follows:

For rendering information and/or providing timely advice: Wayne Akiyama, Lily Burana, Sharon Bradley, Asia Carrera, Philip Cheah, Felix Cheong, Bill Clark, Milena Davidova, Mindy DeBaise, Thierry Delarue, Ben Harrison, Joanna Hughes, Nazir Keshvani, Justin Lam, Lucinda Law, Richard Lim, Steve Lim, Ken Michaels, Raphael Millet, Quill Potter, Grace Quek, Brenda Scofield, Gary See, Steven Shalowitz, Jana Sim, Felix Tan, Trevor Wingert, and Jeff Wozniak.

For reading early drafts and providing invaluable feedback: Helmer Aslaksen, Judy Millar, Samuel Ng, Donald Urquhart, and Kai Vilmi.

For art direction and production assistance: Ming Pang, Jörg Sundermann, Jonathan Ang, Sandy Cheah, Collin Patrick, Maggie Shen, and Mariana Tan.

For visual inspiration: Dana Duncan Seil, from Art Center College of Design in California, whose advice helped with the cover art.

For being the cover model: K.Y., who isn't really an escort but had a blast pretending to be one for a day, in a real hotel suite with real satin sheets.

And for inspiring the title of this book: "Marie from Amsterdam," who showed me just how invisible she is.

As always, I owe a lifelong debt to my literary mentor, the late Bob LaBrasca, who, as my editor at *L.A. Style*, taught me the fine art of magazine writing as cultural anthropology.

I would also like to thank (for various reasons): Victor Bockris, the esteemed author and the first person to persuade me to focus on doing books instead of magazines (and who never forgot to remind me of it every time we met up in New York), Frank Scatoni, my American literary agent (who gave this project his blessing and permitted me the liberty of negotiating the book deal without him), and Peter Schoppert, Managing Director of Singapore University Press, (for his advice on the literary business in Asia and his usual friendship and support).

Finally, words cannot express how grateful I am to my better half, P.H., for enduring nights spent away from home, nights spent toiling at the computer, and nights spent socializing with escorts. Not once did she question my motives, to the amazement of some people. My reputation as a libertine and philanderer has finally, sadly, been put to rest.

Just before he died last year, one of my heroes, the singer-songwriter Warren Zevon, quoted the philosopher Arthur Schopenhauer: "We love to buy books because we believe we're buying the time to read them."

I am hopeful that your time was well spent.

Suggested Reading

Several books served as research sources for this book, and the following are recommended for further reading:

Albert, Alexa. *Brothel: Mustang Ranch and Its Women*. New York: Random House, 2001.

Brazil, David. *No Money, No Honey!: A Candid Look at Sex-for-Sale in Singapore*. 4th ed. Singapore: Angsana Books, 1998.

Brown, Louise. *Sex Slaves: The Trafficking of Women in Asia*. London: Virago Press, 2000.

Burana, Lily. *Strip City: A Stripper's Farewell Journey Across America*. New York: Miramax Books, 2001.

Burdett, John. *Bangkok 8*. New York: Borzoi Books, 2003.

Elias, James E., Vern Bullough, Veronica Elias, and Gwen Brewer (eds.) *Prostitution: On Whores, Hustlers, and Johns*. New York: Prometheus Books, 1998.

Fleiss, Heidi. *Pandering*. Los Angeles: Publishers' Group West, 2003.

Greenfeld, Karl Taro. *Speed Tribes: Days and Nights with Japan's Next Generation*. New York: HarperCollins, 1994.

Greenfeld, Karl Taro. *Standard Deviations: Growing Up and Coming Down in the New Asia*. New York: Villard Books, 2002.

Hollander, Xaviera, with Robin Moore and Yvonne Dunleavy. *The Happy Hooker: My Own Story*. 30th Anniversary Edition. New York ReganBooks, 2002.

McRay, Leslie, with Ted Schwarz. *Kept Women: True Confessions from a Life of Luxury*. New York: Berkley Books, 1992.

Nostitz, Nick. *Patpong: Bangkok's Twilight Zone*. London: Westzone Publishing, 2000.

O'Brian, Martin. *All The Girls*. London: Macmillan, 1982.

Odzer, Cleo. *Patpong Sisters: An American Woman's View of the Bangkok Sex World*. New York: Blue Moon Books, 1994.

Petersen, James R. *The Century of Sex: Playboy's History of the Sexual Revolution, 1900-1999*. New York: Grove Press, 1999.

Quan, Tracy. *Diary of a Manhattan Call Girl*. New York: Crown Publishers, 2001.

Royal, Brandon, and Paul Strahan. *Bars of Steel: The True Story of Marie de la Torre*. Singapore: SNP Editions, 2003.

Taormino, Tristan. *Tristan Taormino's True Lust: Adventures in Sex, Porn and Perversion*. San Francisco: Cleis Press, 2002.

Theroux, Paul. *Saint Jack*. London: Penguin Books, 1976.

Tisdale, Sallie. *Talk Dirty to Me: An Intimate Philosophy of Sex*. New York: Doubleday, 1994.

Warren, James Francis. *Ah Ku and Karayuki-San: Prostitution in Singapore, 1870-1940*. Singapore: Singapore University Press, 2003.

Whitehead, Kate, and Nury Vittachi. *After Suzie: Sex in South China*. Hong Kong: Chameleon Books, 1997.

Permissions

The publisher is grateful for permission to quote from *Days Between Stations* by Steve Erickson©1985 by Steve Erickson, reprinted by permission of Melanie Jackson Agency, LLC; *Journals* by Kurt Cobain, copyright©2001 by The End of Music, LLC, used by permission of Riverhead Books, an imprint of Penguin Group (USA) Inc, and by permission of Viking, an imprint of Penguin Group (UK); *Bangkok 8* by John Burdett©2003 by John Burdett, reprinted by permission of Random House, Inc; 'Leather' by Tori Amos, reprinted by permission of Sword And Stone Publishing, Inc; *Pandering* by Heidi Fleiss©2002 by Heidi Fleiss, reprinted by permission of One Hour Entertainment; *Tristan Taormino's True Lust: Adventures in Sex, Porn and Perversion* by Tristan Taormino©2002 by Tristan Taormino, reprinted by permission of Cleis Press; 'An Embarrassment of Bitches' by Lily Burana©1999by Lily Burana, reprinted by permission of Lily Burana; *Speed Tribes: Days and Nights With Japan's Next Generation* by Karl Taro Greenfeld©1994 by Karl Taro Greenfeld, reprinted by permission of Karl Taro Greenfeld; 'Ann Siang Hill' by Cyril Wong©2002 by Cyril Wong, reprinted by permission of Cyril Wong; and *Saint Jack* by Paul Theroux©1976 by Paul Theroux, reprinted by permission of Paul Theroux.